T0113869

RE-VISION

PURSUING A BETTER VIEW OF GOD'S WAY

LESA D. SHILLING

WestBow Press books may be ordered through booksellers or by contacting:

WestBow Press
A Division of Thomas Nelson & Zondervan
1663 Liberty Drive
Bloomington, IN 47403
www.westbowpress.com
844-714-3454

ISBN: 978-1-6642-8362-6 (sc)
ISBN: 978-1-6642-8363-3 (hc)
ISBN: 978-1-6642-8361-9 (e)

Library of Congress Control Number: 2022920959

Print information available on the last page.

WestBow Press rev. date: 12/09/2022

This book is for all the students who are seeking earnestly for the truth about the big questions of life. Whether you are old or young or somewhere in between, and whether you have been one of my students in-person or are about to become a student under this teaching, I hope you know that I am rooting for you as you ask the hard questions and grapple deeply with knowing Truth. I pray that your heart is open to hearing all the truths presented in these pages so that you can see in a new way, with a new vision for what it means to submit your life to our Great God. To all the students who offered me grace as I did my best to help you navigate into a new vision of God's Truth in your life, thank you. And to all the students who are still struggling to see life from God's perspective, please know my heart yearns for your Re-Vision. I am praying ceaselessly for your ears to hear and your eyes to see the great gift before you.

I John 1:3-4, ESV
That which we have seen and heard, we proclaim also to you, so that you too may have fellowship with us; and indeed, our fellowship is with the Father and with His Son Jesus Christ. And we are writing these things so that our joy may be complete.

1 Corinthians 2:9, ESV
But, as it is written, "What no eye has seen, nor ear heard, nor the heart of man imagined, what God has prepared for those who love Him."

Job 42:5, NLT
I had only heard about you before,
but now I have seen you with my own eyes.

Praying earnestly that your journey through these pages moves you from the delusion of a surface sight to the depths of a stirred soul.

SUGGESTED STUDY PLAN

Week 1: Gather in-person and read Prologue.
Discuss "Prologue" Reflection Questions.
Discuss "Rebuttals and Revisions" Anticipation Questions.
HW: Read "Rebuttals and Revisions" and complete Reflection Questions.

Week 2: Discuss "Rebuttals and Revisions" reading and Reflection Questions.
Read together and discuss Meet Me Here: New Beginnings.
Discuss "A God Like No Other" Anticipation Questions.
HW: Read "A God Like No Other" and complete Reflection Questions.

Week 3: Discuss "A God Like No Other" reading and Reflection Questions.
Read together and discuss Meet Me Here: The Toxic Table.
Discuss "Jesus, Our Greatest Defense" Anticipation Questions.
HW: Read "Jesus, Our Greatest Defense" and complete Reflection Questions.

Week 4: Discuss "Jesus, Our Greatest Defense" reading and Reflection Questions.
Read together and discuss Meet Me Here: E-motions.
Discuss "The Spirit of Fire" Anticipation Questions.
HW: Read "The Spirit of Fire" and complete Reflection Questions.

Week 5: Discuss "The Spirit of Fire" reading and Reflection Questions.
Read together and discuss Meet Me Here: Moving Mountains.
Discuss "Unity of the Trinity" Anticipation Questions.
HW: Read "Unity of the Trinity" and complete Reflection Questions.

Week 6: Discuss "Unity of the Trinity" reading and Reflection Questions.
Read together and discuss Meet Me Here: It's Written in the Sand.
Discuss "Yes, That's the Book for Me" Anticipation Questions.
HW: Read "Yes, That's the Book for Me" and complete Reflection Questions.

Week 7: Discuss "Yes, That's the Book for Me" reading and Reflection Questions.
Read together and discuss Meet Me Here: The Deaner Dis-ease.
Discuss "To Be or Not To Be" Anticipation Questions.
HW: Read "To Be or Not To Be" and complete Reflection Questions.

Week 8: Discuss "To Be or Not To Be" reading and Reflection Questions.
Read together and discuss Meet Me Here: sHe.
Discuss "Speak to Me" Anticipation Questions.
HW: Read "Speak to Me" and complete Reflection Questions.

Week 9: Discuss "Speak to Me" reading and Reflection Questions.
Read together and discuss Meet Me Here: A Recovering Atheist.
Discuss "The Church Lies" Anticipation Questions.
HW: Read "The Church Lies" and complete Reflection Questions.

Week 10: Discuss "The Church Lies" reading and Reflection Questions.
Read together and discuss Meet Me Here: Victims of Love.
Discuss "The Culture Lies" Anticipation Questions.
HW: Read "The Culture Lies" and complete Reflection Questions.

Week 11: Discuss "The Culture Lies" reading and Reflection Questions.
Read together and discuss Meet Me Here: To Hell For Him?.
Discuss "Pain and Purpose" Anticipation Questions.
HW: Read "Pain and Purpose" and complete Reflection Questions.

Week 12: Discuss "Pain and Purpose" reading and Reflection Questions.
Read directions for Meet Me Here: The Story of My Life.
Brainstorm potential ideas for "The Story of My Life" writing assignment.
HW: Read "Epilogue: Where to Now...The Roman Road" and complete "Story of My Life."

Week 13: Discuss the ending and any areas of *Re-Vision* that stood out.
Share "The Story of My Life."
Celebrate the ways God has moved.
Pray for direction for the days to come.

CONTENTS

PROLOGUE

My Dearest Abba Father,

I wish I could pinpoint the first moments of my rendezvous with You, but they began before my feeble memory can recall. I know Your creation speaks in general revelation of all of who you are. I can also look back over the tread marks of these many years and see imprints of my encounters with You there, but I can also see now how limited my vision was for so many years, too many years.

For years, God, I think I may have only caught glimpses of who You really are, and sadly even those snapshots were overshadowed by the many teachings of tradition. I thought I knew You the way all good Christians should know You, until somehow, I woke up one day and realized so many of my visions were founded in false perceptions.

Even good intentions can become putty in the hands of Satan to cast a limited vision of you which propagates into a life still lived for self. In reality, this is also a life lived for Satan even as it looks pristine on the outside with its whitewashed tombs. Church culture never set out to offer a skewed view of You, but I fear too many have failed to show the world the real You, and I am guilty as charged.

God, I don't want to be confined by the past visions cast down to me through generations of beliefs. I want to see You, You in Your full glory, even if it is only as I step out to watch your backside turn the corner of my mountain top experience. God, one moment catching a glimpse of who You really are is worth more than a thousand elsewhere.

So, Lord, I pray that through this endeavor, we will catch just one glimpse. I know that I have tasted and seen Your goodness, and I want absolutely nothing more than to taste again, but what I also really desire is to bring others to the table, a table where all are welcome and nothing matters more than sitting with You, the real You. Not the photoshopped image we have allowed Christian culture to create for the sake of safety. The vast, infinite, dare I say dangerous, You. The You I am seeing more clearly with each new day and can't help but fall in love with...You, only You, the Real You.

My Dearest Unnamed Friend,

This is your invitation to embark on a journey with me and others to see God in a brand-new way. Whether you are like me and think you know Him or are like others you'll meet along this journey who either once entertained thoughts of Him or only know what culture falsely says about Him, you are here for a reason, a God-ordained date if you will. I believe we are all here in this time and space because God wants to open our eyes to see Him in a brand-new way.

Welcome to the quest of Re-Vision.

Reflection Questions:

1. Why are you reading this book?
2. If you had to summarize your current worldview, what would your statement be?
3. How has culture shaped your thinking about God/faith/religion? How has the church shaped your ideas?

ONE

REBUTTALS AND REVISIONS

Anticipation Questions:

1. When you look at the people in your sphere of influence, how would you describe them?
2. What questions about life plague you?
3. Are you a seeker (always asking questions about the realities of life) or a sleeper (content to just go with life as it comes)?

For thirteen years, I taught high school students in the public education system. Although I struggled in my college years to have any clear direction for my life, God took me and led me straight into the teaching field; He knew education is where my skill sets lined up with my heart for loving others which would enable Him to speak into the lives of countless people.

God has worked in the lives of so many for sure because of that path He set me down, but I can't help but always see the one out of the ninety-nine who still needs rescued. I don't know about you, but I see all around me people who simply and desperately need the love of Jesus.

I see students who are caught up in the ranks of status, working tirelessly to fit in and rise to the top of the popularity poll thinking that somehow, when they reach the pinnacle of fame in their measly little high school, they will then feel like they are enough. I watch the way they dress and the way they act and the people they surround themselves with and see how very lost they are. And I want to leave the ninety-nine to come for him; I want to leave the safety of the fold just for her.

I see students who are caught up in the pits of the lowly. They look around and notice how their clothes don't quite measure up or berate themselves because their grades can't quite get there. Never mind the fact that they don't always know where the next meal will come from. Or that home is a far cry from a safe place. Or that tonight may be their lucky night to not be abused in one way or another. Never mind that the lack of foundation may be the very reason they struggle to stay awake in class or find it hard to care about polynomials or participial phrases. I watch the way they either speak too loudly to condemn the "popular" to feel elevated, or they try so hard to shrink into themselves so no one will notice that they don't quite measure up. I can't help but want to find some mode of rescue into their lowly dwellings.

I see adults who are just grown-up versions of these youths. Some adults carry forward the cycle of trying to rise to the top, only to find it comes with a bigger cost. So, the paycheck must escalate to afford keeping up with the Jones's and the stress at home behind closed doors mirrors the surging pace at work, with both spinning out of control. I also see adults who won't look me in the eye or come to events because they deem themselves the untouchables; no one would really want them to come around, only they don't know that I do. I want them to stand a little taller and speak a little louder knowing that they are seen, and they are loved, because just like God would leave the ninety-nine to redeem the lost CEO, He would also leave the ninety-nine for the dumpster diver.

Lately, I have been most saddened, however, by the fine, upstanding citizens who put on their Sunday best once a week to attend a religious event. I guess you could say they go to church, at least that is what most of us here in the Midwest call it, but I think too often they are trading in an authentic experience for a casual encounter. And just like I have said already, it breaks my heart equally for them because they too are lost; they just don't realize it which perhaps makes their situation more dire. We probably won't ask for help if we don't even recognize we are lost.

Everywhere I look are people posing as alive when they are really the walking dead. Jesus says that He is the vine, and we are the branches, and that apart from Him we are dead because He is the source of life. Far too many people whom I love are shriveling up day by day because they have "head knowledge" about who God is or about the role of faith, both believers and nonbelievers alike, but, in reality, they have it all wrong. And if I am honest, I too often have it all wrong.

For years I have asked God to grant direction. What can we do to not only find the lost one but also help him, help her see that He is what they really need? In other words, how can we all get a new vision, a re-vision if you will?

A former student who is still close to me reached out months ago to ask for advice. She had developed a friendship with a young woman over the years, and the two were now best friends. We'll call them Addi and Ellie. So, Addie sends me a text telling me about her friend and how she really needs some resource, a book maybe, that she could use to introduce Christ to her friend. Fast forward to just this last week. Another student is in the middle of a texting conversation and needs advice on where to even start to introduce faith to someone who has no real grasp on faith and may not even really feel the need for it currently in life.

Some of my closest mentorships began under this very premise. The student stood out to me because he or she was a genuine seeker. They didn't want the easy answers to life; they wanted to KNOW. And because they wanted to know, they had done some shopping to find the answers to life's big questions, questions like how we got here, why are we here, is there a God, and if there is, why should I follow Him and not just myself...The questions go on and on. You could google any of those questions and find an overwhelming plethora of proposed answers, so how could anyone figure out the right answer? Is there even a right answer?

I, too, have sought truth for more years than I can now count. When I was little, I would ask my mom "why" about pretty much anything that she dictated, and she often told me, "Because I said so." Now I recognize the much broader rationale for this as a mother of three, but I also know that never cut it for me. I really did want to know the reason; no, I *needed* to know the reason. If you could just give me some rational evidence, a logical explanation, then I could readily follow along, but I struggled with blind faith (and still very much do). So, I started studying, and as I studied in my private life, I found numerous students in my professional life looking for the same answers.

Take Jaxon for instance. Jaxon was starting to consider Christianity until something unraveled his world. As he recovered and put his very talented mind to work, he found numerous philosophies fascinating and could not accept Christianity as the only way. Jaxon's overarching perception of Christianity as an exclusive religion is theologically correct. Jesus says that He is the Way, the only way. But maybe there is more than meets Jaxon's eye…

Maybe there is more than meets your eyes too. Maybe there is more than meets my eyes. Maybe that is the very point. Maybe we don't fully see even as we all are grasping for clearer vision. 1 Corinthians 2:9 (NLT) says, "No eye has seen, no ear has heard, no mind has conceived what God has prepared for those who love him." Paul is quoting Isaiah 64:4 (NIV) which says, "Since ancient times no one has heard, no ear has perceived, no eye has seen any God besides you, who acts on behalf of those who wait for Him." Both verses imply that we can never fully understand God, but what do we learn when we compare the two or evaluate them in context?

First, let's compare. Both state no one has seen/perceived, and no one has heard, but what has no one seen or heard? Paul says we cannot conceive what God has prepared for his followers. This would imply we cannot imagine how great "heaven" will be. Isaiah, in contrast, says that we have not perceived any God who can compare to our God because He is a God who acts on behalf of those who wait for Him. This seems richer, fuller in detail. It reminds us that if we want to follow Him, we must wait on Him and not rush ahead of Him; we cannot follow if we are leading. And if we wait on Him to lead us, He promises to act on our behalf and grant us blessings, which is an overarching theme in Old Testament covenant promises. So, Paul's version says we can never fully comprehend what God is preparing for those of us who love Him. Isaiah's version reminds us that we can find no one who compares to our God because He is acting on behalf of those who want to follow Him and not lead the way on their own. Overall, both imply our inability to fully comprehend, but the _____ that we are comprehending varies a bit.

Let's take Isaiah in context a little more. Isaiah spends the beginning of the chapter talking about the mighty ways God shows His power. He discusses how God does awesome things we never expected which is why no one, since ancient times, has ever seen a God quite like the one they are now seeing. For the first time, they are seeing God in a new way because they are seeing His power on display.

Look at 1 Corinthians 2:9 (NIV) and read on. Right after Paul references the Isaiah verse, he writes, "But God has revealed it to us by His Spirit." Stop. . . Soak that in. Isaiah urges us to know that until we stop to see God and His power on display, we will never conceive Him to the depths of His nature. Paul says we also struggle to comprehend the vastness of our God, BUT, and the but is huge, we now can because God has revealed it to us through His Spirit.

What do Jaxon and all the lost have in common? They see everything from their own vantage point. Ever since Pentecost, God has offered His very Spirit for those who will submit to Him, and with His Spirit comes the ability to KNOW. I love Jaxon dearly. He is intensely smart, super fun, and an amazing young person who means so very much to me, enough that I would leave the ninety-nine.

I get why so many think the way they do; they don't have spiritual eyes. Every time they process a thought or consider an action, it is done from the vantage point of me, myself, and I. And although their hearts cry out for justice (which stems from the fact that they were made in the image of the very one who is the epitome of justice), they still fall short of truth because their perception is jaded. Their eyes cannot see, their ears cannot hear, their mind cannot conceive how God works because they view everything through the material lens of self.

Years ago, a theory called Relativism entered the world. Relativism proposes that moral truth is relative to each member of humanity, therefore no absolute moral truth exists. Relativism took the concept of universal right and wrong and traded it in for self-discernment. If I think it is right for me, then it is right. If I think it is wrong for me, then it is wrong. I could give a rather long lecture on the faulty ground this theory stands upon, but for now, let's consider where that theory leads.

A wise writer once said that before she makes any decision, before she jumps into any river, she walks alongside it first to see where it will likely take her. She knows that once she jumps in, the current will be too strong to go any direction but down that river.[1] Let's apply that "truth" here. If we jump in the river of relativism, where does that lead?

First, let's make it clear that I do not live on a mountain in complete seclusion. This means I am never fully free to do anything I like because my actions will have ripple effects on those who live within my sphere of influence. The only way to have a fully free will is to either be God himself (but even He is willing to let our requests shift the trajectory of outcomes...i.e., Sodom and Gomorrah), or be in a world where there is no God, no people, and no environment, which just means you aren't existing. Even if you lived on a mountain where your choices did not impact others, you still have nature surrounding you. Your choices impact it and the effects of nature impact you, hence you aren't fully free to do whatever you want, however you want, whenever you want. We are always living under a limited free will.

But we do have some autonomy over our decisions, so with that being noted, let's flow down the river of relativism with our other people who are doing life in our sphere and with nature equally impacting us. Hypothetically speaking, let's take a trip down river. First, I decide I want to have a super fun ride, so I create lots of waves. What I don't realize is that one of those waves capsized the boat with a baby, and he drowned. Tomorrow, I decide I want to eat peanut butter, so I gobble up my sandwich and then share the peanut butter with a neighbor who

---

[1] Terkeurst, Lysa. "Read This Before Making That Decision." *Proverbs 31 Ministries*, 13 June 2019, https://proverbs31.org/read/devotions/full-post/2019/06/13/read-this-before-making-that-decision.

is deathly allergic. So, life is not going so swell for me because I now have two angry neighbors, grieving severe losses. They decide it feels most right to destroy my boat in retaliation which means I am still alive since I can swim, but exhausted and not enjoying life. I then decide to hop on ship with the next person who floats along, but I didn't realize that they have decided they can't stand wet people (they have a right to personal prejudice), so they grab their knife. Let's just say that is the end of my story in the river.

The story is obviously exaggerated, but one problem with relativism is injustice. So then maybe we just need to move toward collective agreement to discern right from wrong. Even that holds troublesome outcomes; if the majority decides a certain people group should die, then it is off with their heads. Just ask the French how that worked out for them. Can you sense the dilemma? Without a moral code that originates beyond the human sphere, all life leads to chaos and destruction for anyone not in the majority because we are forever doomed to see things only from our own limited perspective.

What if we replaced the relativism plan with a redemption plan, one that said there is absolute truth, and it comes from an external source; His name is God. He offers a code of right and wrong and a way to be redeemed from the wrongs we commit. He also offers His very Spirit to take up residence in us so that we can begin to conceive His ways, His fame, His power, His viewpoint.

Without him, we are forever enslaved to our limited perceptions. Jaxon has a really good heart and great intentions, but his viewpoint is limited. The good man who goes to church every Sunday is the same; he has a good heart and good intentions, but even his viewpoint is limited. We all live under limitations of our perceptions, but we don't have to stay that way. We can choose a new pair of glasses and see things every day in a brand-new way, learning more today than we knew the day before, seeing reality more and more clearly with each passing day.

We each have limited perception while also living under limited free will because God's will always trumps ours, but in that free will comes the ability to make the most important decision in our lives. Will we choose to follow God and see life His way and be radically redeemed, or will we choose to follow self and see life our own way and be relatively destroyed?

My prayer is that you will at least entertain some further reading. I mean, it never hurts to just walk alongside the river of faith for a bit to see where the water leads. Who knows? You may even decide it really is best to get wet.

Reflection Questions:

1. How can we know truth/Truth?
2. How does living for "self" differ from living for God?
3. Are we ever truly free to do as we want, how we want, when we want? Why or why not?
4. How are our perceptions limited?

Meet Me Here

-New Beginnings-

You find me.

I like to think I am good at hiding. That in the depths of my drawing inward I really can escape your notice. But who do I think I am fooling? You always know.

You know me when I lie down and when I arise. You see all my failures and flaws.

Today I am feeling the pits of failed despair…

Swirling and twirling all around me, echoes of whatifs, shouldve, couldve, wouldve, and a prominent noise reminding me of my incessant ignorance.

In my mind I imagine I can halt the noise. I picture me sitting in the midst of a large arena full of the smells of turf, city air, dirt and grime… and all around me spins an intensity of otherness…people, noises, commotion, chaos… I feel all closing in around me but in a moment's breath, I exhale a small wisp of you, and suddenly it all vanishes. Whoosh…gone.

I am perplexed and a bit unsettled. The sudden dizziness of a world spinning stopped, and I am trying to regain my bearings. Out of the corner of my eye I sense motion, so I shift my focus to the far corner of the field. I can make out someone moving into focus, walking towards me. Steadied gaze intently peering into me, I watch you as you make your way to my side.

By this time, my breathing is labored, and my heart is pounding. I may be having an anxiety attack for fear of the unknown. I want to look away, to peer down at my dirty shoes, but your eyes are fixed on mine, and I cannot budge them even as I try. You hold me steady even while all within feels like it is flying apart.

Slowly, deliberately, almost before I realize what has happened, you reach out and take my hand. I recognize that in my mind I can halt the noise, but in reality, I can never halt You.

You always know.

You know every part of me, every doubt I don't declare, every fear I don't face, every misgiving I misplace.

The palm of your hand is warm. Not a sticky kind of touch, but a smooth, soft sliding into mine kind of reach. And as you lift my wearied soul from the cold earth, I sense something new is about to begin.

Something new always begins with You.

TWO

A GOD LIKE NO OTHER

Anticipation Questions:

1. What are three things you "know" about God?
2. Who or what has helped you better know God?
3. Who or what has made you distant from God?
4. What arguments do you possibly have for not following God?

When I was a little girl, we would get to go to the basement for kids' church to encounter God. Low vaulted ceilings with an aisle spread smally between two rows of pews became the place where I was first taught the character of God.

I learned that God is in control. I was told that God loves me. I heard stories through songs about the God who saw Zacchaeus and told him to come down because God had a different plan for his life or about the little light that God placed inside me that I should not hide under a bushel. I learned through the years that followed those infant teachings that God expected me to do the right things. If I wanted to be a good Christian, I should offer prayers to Him, read my Bible, attend church if the doors were open, and follow the rules.

In other words, I learned that I should be a good citizen who also paid lip-service to God while being present in a building called His house, but the honest truth is it always felt like I was invading someone else's space. God's house never felt like my own. So, I got good at masquerades. I played the part well while I slowly drifted through lots of unsettled seasons in my heart. Eventually even my personal life drifted from faith as it played out through the week, becoming my own space to try to figure out who I was. That life was a far cry from someone who knew God intimately.

I should certainly pause at this moment and say it was not fully my church's fault that I had misperceived the reality of God and what it meant to be His. I can now readily pinpoint people who were living out the faith well, but most of my encounters were knee deep at best, and what I really craved was authentic immersion. I never was one to just wade into something half-heartedly, so my experience with God felt a bit fake, as if my only expectations were to look good on the outside while all within me cried for something real.

I don't know where you are in your own walk, but I do know you picked up this book for some reason or another. I guess I just want to be honest from the start that even now I am still pulling back layers of false perception as each day brings new light to who God really is. If you want in on a secret.... each day finds me more and more exhilarated by the new ways I am seeing God, catching more and more glimpses of who He really is and how much I need to re-vision the character of my great, great God.

The God Who Loves Me, Not Himself:

Many years ago, much before I was prepared to give an answer, a student who knew I was a Christian challenged me about the nature of God. She asked me, "Why in the world would I want to worship a narcissistic God who created me just so I could spend my life worshiping Him?"

The question caught me off guard, and I had no answer. I went home and grappled with that question and still concluded nothing worthy of rebuttal. Years later, as I began this journey of peeling back the false layers so I could start to see God for who He really is, I realized the crutch of her argument. You see, I knew God did indeed create me so I could bring Him glory and honor through my worship of Him. In that part, she was so correct. I knew in my heart that God was not a narcissist, but I could not reconcile the two. Then I asked myself this question, "Does God ***need*** me to worship Him?"

The answer is no. A narcissist demands attention to feed an ego, but if God is who He says He is, He is already complete and full and whole and all that and then some with or without me, with or without all of humanity. And if God does not need me to worship Him for His sake, then the only other option is that He needs me to worship Him for *my sake*.

So why would I need to worship God for my sake? In this life, we all have two options. We can live for "self" (the flesh), or we can live for God (the spirit). Romans talks a lot about this. We can either spend a lifetime limited by the worship of our little hobgoblin minds that are finite, mortal, and of no lasting importance, OR we can spend a lifetime of endless opportunities by worshipping the God of all creation who is infinite, immortal, and holds all purpose for all mankind. And then I realized the conundrum of her question. The problem was not with God wanting us to worship Him; the problem was with the motive. In her mind, God's motive was self-gratification, yet God's completeness could never be increased by my measly affection. BUT my measly existence can readily be increased when aligned with His infinite I Am. So, He did it all just for me; He did it all just for you.

The Life Giver:

When I reached the age of making my own decisions and launching into my own "coming of age" journey, my parents made it very clear what I was and was not allowed to do. Church teaching, at least in my mind, played the same tune. I saw the Bible as a list of dos and don'ts, and as I looked around at most of the people of all ages who attended church with me, I did not encounter authentic transformations, but rather people who were also following the set rules. They attended church and even served in various ways, but their weeks were spent living a rather worldly life. For sure, they were good moral people, but good moral people go to hell all the time. I did not encounter a church full of people who were ON

MISSION DAILY for God's kingdom, and that simply didn't align with the people I read about in God's story. So instead, it seemed to me that my job was to follow the rules without any need to live a life that would in any way model the lives of those talked about in the Bible.

God's intent was not to find humans who would follow the law; God's intent was to find humans who would follow Him. Scripture makes it very clear that God sent His own son Jesus because the set of rules, the law, could never adequately transform us or redeem us. Romans 3:20-24 (NIV) says:

> "Therefore no one will be declared righteous in his sight by observing the law; rather, through the law we become conscious of sin. But now a righteousness from God, apart from law, has been made known, to which the Law and the Prophets testify. This righteousness from God comes through faith in Jesus Christ to all who believe. There is no difference, for all have sinned and fall short of the glory of God and are justified freely by His grace through the redemption that came by Christ Jesus."

God's word tells us time and again that we could never be justified in His sight by simply following the rules. If we break just one rule we are doomed, condemned to a life apart from God which is the very definition of Hell itself. So, from the beginning, all the way back to Genesis 1 where Elohim (a plural word proving Jesus is already there) sits in creation, Jesus was part of God's plan, a plan that never intended us to see Him strictly as a rule-giver. God, my friend, is a life-giver.

A BIG GOD:

Howard G. Hendricks once said, "The size of your God determines the size of everything."[2] The bigness of God begs our attention as a launching point for understanding who He really is.

---

[2] "Howard Hendricks Tribute." *Dallas Theological Seminary*, https://www.dts.edu/howard-hendricks-tribute/.

Years ago, my husband and I were watching some faith-based movies with our kids on a regular basis. The Kendrick brothers' movies became some of our favorites, and I can recount conversations with my kids explaining to them that the supernatural things that happened in those stories really were very possible in their own lives. Too often, children grow up reading stories in the Bible and write them off as fairytales of their childhood imaginations, but GOD DID THOSE THINGS THEN AND HE STILL DOES THEM NOW. Yet too many of us sit in the comforts of our "Christian" cultures with no expectation for God to do supernatural things, somehow forgetting that God Himself IS SUPERNATURAL.

So, when I started on this journey of re-visioning God's character, I started asking Him to show up in supernatural ways that would force me to refute any other explanations. And you know what? HE DID. Want to know something even more incomprehensible? He wants to do the same for you.

An Immanent God:

When we think of God's bigness, we think of Him as Elohim, a transcendent God who is omnipotent, powerful enough to do all things imaginable and more importantly, all things beyond our wildest dreams. This is the God we see outlined from the very beginning of scripture in Genesis 1.

In Genesis 2, we hear the same creation story again, only from a different angle, and it is in this recapitulation (recap) of the story that we see the Immanent God, the God who walks within the story too.[3] The omni word for this characteristic of God is omnipresent. I grew up hearing these omni words and as a geeky intellectual, I clung to them thinking they were cool without ever pondering the depths of what they conveyed about God's character.

Foremost, God's omnipresence means he transcends time. Okay, cool, right? Nope...this is way more than cool and deserves some attention.

---

3 Myers, Jeff. *Understanding the Faith: A Survey of Christian Apologetics.* Summit Ministries, 2016.

God stands in all times at all times. . . Let me say that again. God is standing in the year 2000 BC in this moment while also standing in the year 2000 AD. And He consecutively is standing in every single moment of every single day of all "time" that has already transpired on this earth while also standing in every single moment of every single day of all "time" yet to come. This ability to transcend time also then means He is omniscient, or all-knowing. That in itself is a conversation for an entirely different book as we then try to process how a God who can know all things still offers us free will, but for now, suffice to say, God's ability to transcend time while maintaining humanity's free will may seem difficult for our limited minds to grasp, but it is a walk in the park for a big God.

If we rest on the promise that God's character enables Him to move unbounded by time and space, we come to realize that we cannot hide from Him. One of my favorite songs that embraces God's presence was penned by Sarah Reeves. In her song "Nowhere," she says, "There's nowhere that I can go. There's nowhere that I can hide. When I feel like I'm alone, Your love and my heart collide." The psalmist writes it well when he says in Psalms 139:1-5a, 7-10 (NIV):

> "O Lord, you have searched me, and You know me. You know when I sit and when I rise; you perceive my thoughts from afar...You hem me in-behind and before...Where can I go from Your Spirit? Where can I flee from Your Presence? If I go up to the heavens, you are there; if I make my bed in the depths, you are there. If I rise on the wings of the dawn, if I settle on the far side of the sea, even there Your hand will guide me, Your right hand will hold me fast."

My friend, God surrounds you even in this moment. Even if you have never invited Him to sit at your table, He is nearby, waiting earnestly to have dinner with you. Even if you have sat with Him for years but have given over His seat to the enemy, He awaits you yet. And even if you have been dining with Him for quite some time, He still yearns to reveal more of himself to You.

You simply cannot escape a God who exists in all times, at all times, and permeates the very air you breathe.

You see, in Genesis 2, God retells the story from a relational angle. Instead of highlighting the things he made, he takes the camera and zooms in on his special creation, the part made in His image. Focusing on Adam and Eve, God retells the story from an immanent angle, demonstrating how far He would go just to be with us. So, God himself comes into the garden to do life with them. And though God can no longer walk the paths of the garden with you and me, He went even further to walk the road to Calvary with you in His very mind, and then sent His very Spirit to live inside you.

He loves you that much….

The transcendent God who holds all power and authority and honor and glory became immanent so he could dwell within our world just so He could walk with you and me as we travel this journey called life. You must know, beyond a shadow of a doubt, that this God is a God of abounding love who yearns to be with you every step of the way.

A Dangerous God:

The Chronicles of Narnia capture the essence of God through the lead character, a lion named Aslan. Reading these books have been one more piece to my journey of seeing God differently, and one of my absolute favorite parts comes in the story *The Lion, The Witch, and The Wardrobe.* Little Lucy questions Mr. Beaver about this lion named Aslan, asking if he is safe. Mr. Beaver replies that God is not safe, but He is the King and He is good, a great reminder that life is meant to be beyond our control. [4]

For most mediocre Christians, life trudges along with no need for a King to lead them into the battle of life where they adventure far beyond the safety of camp. In turn, the concept of God as dangerous seems a bit "wild" to them, and rightfully so. If you have never lived a life beyond your own abilities, you have never found the need for a God beyond the size of

---

[4] Lewis, C.S. *The Chronicles of Narnia.* The Signature Ed., HarperCollins, 1978.

your comfortable box. But, if you have lived a life following God into the unknown, you will soon come to realize that He never promises safety.

When I presented this to a group of jr. high students, I realized after conversations with parents that this was a difficult concept for them to grasp. I can readily excuse developing youth, but if I am honest, I struggle to offer the same patience to mature adults. What exactly does a dangerous God mean then for us who are intellectually mature enough for this level of critical thinking. Does God want us to live endangered lives?

I believe the answer is yes, but not necessarily in the context of how our culture would define danger. Does God want us to haphazardly risk our physical lives every day in the name of Him for no apparent reason? I don't recall a commandment that says, "Thou shalt walk out on a busy highway everyday of your existence." I do, however, recall countless stories where Paul's life was endangered. In fact, I think it is no coincidence that all of Jesus's disciples died a martyr's death except John, but even John was persecuted and exiled to the island of Patmos.

Do I think God is asking me to purposely put myself in harm's way today? Not necessarily. I don't see Paul or Stephen or any of the others out looking for trouble. I do, however, see that they were out serving faithfully which meant they would inevitably encounter obstacles that required God to go before them and behind them and in them. I think God asks the same of me, and I think He asks the same of you. If we are living within our own means, we are living within our own safety. If we are living beyond ourselves by living for Him, on mission, with sights set on doing whatever He asks of me, He will ask me to step out on the water. He will insist that I trust Him to take care of me even as my surroundings crash around me, demanding I leave the safety of the boat.

Mr. Beaver says it well when he reminds us that God is not safe, but He is good, AND all that rests on the fact that He is king. Living a life in the arms of God will mean danger lies ahead, danger defined as being out of our control. But more important than the danger is the goodness of God. He promises He will never leave us nor forsake us, and as the King of all creation who holds all power and dominion and glory and honor, we can trust Him to take care of us spiritually, knowing that our physical bodies are just temporary.

The God Who Won't Forsake:

Forsaken synonyms include words like abandon, desert, reject, disown…As Jesus hangs on the cross for your sins and mine, He cries out to His Father. Matthew 27:46 (NIV) says, "About three in the afternoon, Jesus cried out in a loud voice 'Eli, Eli, lema sabachthani?' (which means 'My God, my God, why have you forsaken me?')". Jesus faced complete abandonment from God, and the only other people who will face the same are those who choose hell.

Hell by its very description is an absence of God. Because God IS all good things, being completely separated from Him, completely disowned, rejected, deserted, abandoned by the One who IS all Good, means only evil will remain. Some may argue that God sends people to hell, but scripture consistently proves that even as God foreknows our choices, He still allows us free will to choose our destiny.

If you choose to submit your life to Christ, allowing His sacrifice to take your place of rejection, you will live eternally in God's presence because He promises to never leave us nor forsake us. When Moses is about to die, he reminds the Israelites that, "The Lord your God goes with you; He will never leave you nor forsake you" (Deuteronomy 31:6, NIV). The writer of Hebrews echoes this same sentiment, that God will not forsake us which means we can confidently know that we have nothing to fear because "What can man do to me?" (Hebrews 13: 5-6, ESV). Honestly, man can certainly make you feel miserable here on earth…. if you allow them a voice into your life. But if you choose daily to live under the protection of the God who promises to NEVER forsake you, to never abandon you, then you truly have NOTHING to fear, my friend, absolutely nothing.

The God who is I AM:

When Moses comes before God terrified by the task set before him, he asks God for His name. God, knowing the deep importance of names in the Jewish culture, tells Moses that His name is I Am. I absolutely love that God made it clear from the earliest days that any attempt to define Him will always fall short of who He really is.

As I grew up in the church, I did not see God this way. I saw Him in limited perspectives, hindering my ability to see why I really could live for Him. But the truth, my friend, is that God has always been and will always be much more than we could ever express with our mere words. And because He is the great I Am, I will never face a day where I have come to the end of my quest for knowing Him more, and neither will you. Each day when the sun peaks its face into the corners of our curtains, God offers a new opportunity to see him and know Him a little more than we did the day before. I hope that is something that drives you from your bed each day, the promise of getting a better glimpse of the God who beckons us to follow Him as he rounds the corner of the mountain summit that He is inviting us to explore.

So, who is this God who beckons us? He is the creator of all things, and that includes you. He is the sustainer of all things, the provider of all things, the protector of all things, the healer of all things, the life-giver to all things, and the list could go on and on. The point is this: God is all things. If you don't have Him in your life, then your life is not just lacking some things, it is lacking all things.

Your life is null and void without Him.

Reflection Questions:

1. Of all these attributes of God, which one spoke to you the most? Why?
2. Which one is the hardest for you to believe? Why?
3. Why do we settle for safe lives?
4. What is one thing God is asking you to believe and then act upon?

Meet Me Here

-The Toxic Table-

The table sits broad and inviting upon the thrust of civilization. I could try to count the chairs at her beckoning, but they seem to elude any attempt. Heavy-laden oak, they house creatures of all shapes and sizes.

I see an old man sitting next to his wife. She helps him read his bible because he can no longer see for himself, but the vision of his mind sees into the heart of God. Through the blackened flaws of his life, he has remained faithful to seeking. He seeks well.

I see a young woman. Beautiful and elegant, she shyly comes toward one of the chairs. She slowly takes her hand from her pocket, and I can't help but notice it is shaking. The glint of unworthiness shades her countenance and I know she is afraid.

I too have been afraid. Afraid of what may happen if I come to the table. Will they let me sit and dine with them? Am I really invited to partake of this great banquet? Could they really accept me if they knew the truth? If somehow I must present the damnable shames that have colored my past, would they accept me for who I am, without one plea?

The young woman starts to walk away, but the man can hear her nervous breathing. He reaches out toward her. As his wrinkly, clotted, scraggly fingers touch the youthy flesh of her smooth forearm, she startles back. The last time someone touched her was lethal. But she soon settles, recognizing the warmth that permeates to her soul because of his one kind gesture to invite her to sit with him a spell.

I am suddenly encouraged. Maybe I too could join that party. Maybe I too could be enough.

Then I see a figure approach the table. IT stands tall and steady. ITs voice speaks boldly. IT claims ITs space at one of the heads and pulls the oak chair out with authority to sit down.

A voice from afar breaks into the silence as He approaches IT. "My dearest child. For today, that is not your spot. I have reserved that for a special guest."

Taken aback, IT can't help but question even as IT grants full acknowledgement towards the approaching man. "But Father. You know my deeds. You know how I read your word and falter not from any accordance you have mandated. You know how I have served you."

"Yes, my child. I know. But remember too that I love all my creatures, great and small. For the last shall be first and the first shall be last. You know that many are called but few are chosen. Today, I do not choose you."

IT struggles to catch its breath. How could he not choose IT?

"Child, you are more than welcome at the table, always, and certainly a day may come when that seat is yours, but for today, it is for her."

He steadies his glance at me.

"For her. Why, do you know what she is? Do you know she lives a pretentious life shaded with uncountable sins? I have never missed a single decree. You owe me my due process."

"Child, your due process is hell. My grace alone sets you free. She has sought refuge in me, and she will have it. My son's sacrifice reshades her shame more than it could ever whitewash your tomb."

Even as He speaks, I feel my knees give way. How can he possibly ask me to even sit at the table, much less at the head opposite of Him?

"Oh, dearest Father, I cannot." And as the words somehow falter out, I begin to weep uncontrollably. Before my eyes flash the countless sins of my past, and I sink further into the pit of me.

I then feel him coming close to me. I feel his hand under my arm as he lifts me from the mire and gives me a new identity. As he leads me toward the chair, I immediately notice that IT was standing farther away, having recoiled in seeming frustration about the course of events.

I look into my Father's eyes, and then toward IT, and I cannot help but notice the pain in IT's eyes, so I beg, "Lord, please. Can't IT come too?"

He lovingly smiles at IT, whose eyes were intently watching him. "All are welcome at my table."

I look, and I lock eyes with IT. Somehow in the depths of me, I plead that IT will come and join us in our feast. I know the atrocities that await outside the presence of this place. Would IT humble ITs heart and stay?

For a moment I think IT is coming. But then, over the course of the next few minutes, I see an army slowly rise behind, and then they boldly, loudly proclaim that we are all chasing shadows; don't we know that God calls the morally righteous and not the sinners become saints.

Fear sweeps over me as I fix my eyes upon Jesus who is now seated at the right hand of God. If this is true, then I will be thrown out from this place into the weeping and gnashing of teeth. I had lived a life of hell on earth and wished not to revisit such a joyless place.

Jesus stands and walks over to me. Placing a hand on my shoulder, he looks up at IT and ITs host of complaints. A tear slides down his face. "Dearest one, you cannot fly in the face of the gospels and choose which parts to believe. Believe them all or believe them not. The choice has always been yours. But as for my table, you will not turn it toxic."

All rests upon this moment. Will IT submit to the authority of Christ or will IT rest assured in ITs own false morality built on man's precepts?

I can see IT hesitate. The longer IT hesitates, the more ITs army seems dismayed, until finally, one of them stands.

"That table is toxic. I will not partake of its bread and wine without man sitting at the head of its meditation."

Soon, the other soldiers begin to rise and gain volume until finally IT had a choice. Rebuke ITs army or lead them.

As IT chooses the latter, I weep once again. And so does Jesus.

THREE

JESUS, OUR GREATEST DEFENSE

Anticipation Questions:

1. What do you appreciate about Jesus?
2. Why does belief in Jesus matter?
3. What questions perplex you when it comes to Jesus?

If you have run church circles much at all, you have heard of the Trinity. We will get to a chapter on that concept later, but seekers coming to the table asking basic answers about faith want to know about God, Jesus, and the Holy Spirit. They have questions about each separately and then also how the Godhead, three in one, operates. The second piece to that puzzle is Jesus Christ; understanding the role Jesus plays in the faith world is crucial for a bigger reason than you may currently realize.

Let's start with the parts you may have heard. Foremost, Jesus is God's only son born of the virgin Mary. Why is it so important that he was birthed by a virgin? This very aspect of his coming to earth asserts his divinity, a premise we will continue to build as we investigate his character. Jesus did have an earthly father who was Mary's husband;

Joseph played a role in the upbringing of Jesus to some degree at least, even though scripture tells us very little. Mary enters scripture more than Joseph, but even information about her relationship with Jesus is limited to various appearances as Jesus is a young boy, and then occasionally, she appears during his ministry period. Why does any of this matter? The bible's lack of information about them reminds us that Jesus grew up under the shadow and guidance of the Most High God.

But wait, isn't He fully God and fully man? Yes. As fully God, he gave up his right to be in Heaven so that He could be present among us for the sake of setting the ultimate example of the life we should strive to lead while limited to a physical body here on earth. So, in his full humanity, He suffered and struggled with the earthly woes we all face so that He could become the ultimate sacrifice and pay the price once and for all. When God sees those of us who have accepted Jesus as the Lord of our lives and are covered by the grace of His blood, God only sees our holiness. By going to the cross, Jesus became fully forsaken by God himself while He hung on that cross, a loneliness you and I never have to experience if we choose submission while we live here on earth.

A young girl in Kids Worship once asked me why there had to be a sacrifice; why couldn't God just speak the words of salvation and it happen, just like when God spoke the whole world into existence. I believe we must first understand that everything God created demonstrates his order of the universe and the precepts He has instilled in this order of life. For example, when God rests on the seventh day, He is establishing a precept of rest that is needed for mankind to live healthy lives. When God established justice as a precept, He established the need for something to be sacrificed for payment of deserved wrath. In the Old Testament, priests offered numerous sacrifices; in the New Testament covenant, Jesus came to be the perfect sacrifice once and for all. God obviously wants us to understand that all things come with a price, and the price for our redemption costs more than we could imagine.

So we have this Jesus figure who was born of a virgin, raised under God's authority, lived a fully human life even as he maintained his full divinity, faced rejection by God as He hung on a cross, and was forsaken as He took our sins upon his shoulders so that by His wounds we would be healed. He paid the ultimate price just so you could stand before God without punishment for the sins you will commit even as you offer your life in submission. Pretty amazing character in this story, ey? I mean what more could matter than who Jesus is?

The storyline of Jesus certainly explodes on the pages of our own life stories, but the real crux of his story is its apologetic proof.

Let me ask a question? If someone wanted to doubt the Christian worldview, what would they most need to disprove? They wouldn't need to deny the existence of a God because numerous worldviews support belief in a god or gods. They wouldn't need to deny the existence of a historically accurate text because numerous religions have their own version of a bible. They wouldn't feel threatened to deny the existence of the Holy Spirit since His very nature and role are more obscure and subjective in the first place. The character of Jesus, however, and claims of his death and resurrection establish Christianity as a testament quite different from all the others; hence understanding not only who Jesus is but also why His story is crucial for defense of the Christian faith propels this worldview into a category all on its own.

Lee Strobel was an atheist journalist who set out to discredit Christianity. His research eventually pointed him toward the resurrection. If he could disprove this one event, then all of Christianity's claims would crumble. You know what He discovered? All evidence pointed to a resurrection.[5]

Entire books have been written about this very topic, and you should certainly read them. To help introduce you to the major concepts, let's consider Josh and Sean McDowell's major points covered in *More Than a Carpenter.*

Point 1: Did Jesus really live? We won't go into any details here, but there is more historical evidence for the life of Jesus than your life by far, and do you exist here on planet earth?

Point 2: Some non-believers project the argument that they can fully recognize Jesus as a historical figure, a good man who lived on

---

[5] Strobel, Lee. *The Case for Christ: A Journalist's Personal Investigation of the Evidence for Jesus.* Zondervan, 2016.

this earth, but He was not God's son; He was just a good teacher. Josh points out that Jesus is either Lord, Liar, or Lunatic. Consider this; Jesus fully claimed to be God's son, and who in their right mind would say a good moral teacher spent his entire ministry professing a lie? Perhaps he only said those things because He was delusional; so now we have a lunatic. The choice then is either Jesus was an insane man who falsely believed He was divine; Jesus was a liar and hence not a good moral teacher; or Jesus was who He said He was, Lord of all creation.

Point 3: A basic premise of science says the only way to prove a theory is to be able to repeat it through a scientifically controlled experiment. Since we can't replicate Jesus's life since that moment in history is gone, we must rely on the legal-historical proof of oral and written testimonies and exhibits. We have numerous oral and written testimonies documented throughout the Bible that prove Jesus was who He said He was, but then how do we trust the historicity of the Bible. Can we prove the Bible is a reliable document? Do just a basic Google search and you will quickly find there is more evidence for the authenticity of the Bible as a historical document than any other document preserved from ancient times.

Point 4: Speaking of testimonies brings us to a discussion of his followers. After Jesus rose from the dead, hundreds profess they saw Him. Not only were they saying they saw Him, but they were also meeting martyrs' deaths left and right because they refused to go back on their word. If Jesus had not risen from the dead, this conspiracy would have at least eventually fallen flat because who really wants to die for a lie?

Point 5: Speaking of lies, numerous intellectuals have proposed alternate solutions to the empty tomb. Maybe they moved the body? Maybe they got the wrong tomb? Maybe the body was stolen? Maybe Jesus just swooned and then came back to life and was able to walk out of the tomb? The list goes on, and rational rebuttals easily explain why these lies do not hold up under attack.

Point 6: Jesus fulfilled approximately 300 prophecies if we include all prophetic statements and "address" stamps of the Messiah. The probability of fulfilling just forty-eight is 1 in 10 to the 157th power.

Some of those prophecies were beyond his ability to fulfill; for example, as a baby, he had no say over where and how He was born.

Point 7: Saul was ruthlessly attacking Christians and almost overnight became Christ's most loyal and passionate advocate. Consider also how much He suffered for this transformation. 2 Corinthians 11: 24-28 (NIV) says:

> "Five times I received from the Jews the forty lashes minus one. Three times I was beaten with rods, once I was pelted with stones, three times I was shipwrecked, I spent a night and a day in the open sea, I have been constantly on the move. I have been in danger from rivers, in danger from bandits, in danger from my fellow Jews, in danger from Gentiles, in danger in the city, in danger in the country, in danger at sea; and in danger from false believers. I have labored and toiled and have often gone without sleep; I have known hunger and thirst and have often gone without food; I have been cold and naked. Besides everything else, I face daily the pressure of my concern for all the churches."

Saul indeed must have had some radical encounter on the road to Damascus to have been so completely transformed and devoted for years to the call from Christ.

Point 8: Do you personally know someone who just seems to be at peace even as life is full of turmoil? Have you ever met someone who just seems to overflow naturally with joy? Have you ever wondered where that could possibly come from? Transformations in God's people who walk the earth even today are further evidence for the Case for Christ.[6]

---

6 McDowell, Josh, and Sean McDowell. *More Than a Carpenter.* Tyndale Momentum, 2009.

I AM:

In the book of John, Jesus gives several "I Am" statements that can help us further understand the very character of Jesus and why He is so crucial to our own life narratives. In John 6:35 (NIV), Jesus tells us that He is the bread of life. Have you ever craved fulfillment? Have you ever sought the world over for something that brings lasting contentment only to wake up the next day and still feel a little empty? Would you believe me if I told you it doesn't have to be this way? Jesus promises to fill us to the full so that we will never be hungry again because He can satisfy our deepest yearnings.

John 8:12 (NIV) says, "I am the light of the world. Whoever follows me will not walk in darkness but will have the light of life." When I was a little girl, I was terrified of being alone in the dark, and if I am honest, it still intimidates me. I was convinced something would get me. And then God got me, and I realized I don't have to be afraid of the things I can't see. You see, oftentimes it is not the physical dark we fear, but rather the future dark we can't foresee. Jesus promises to shine light into all dark places if we only follow Him. We will never have to walk alone through the valley of shadows because He really does go with us and in us. And in case you have never stopped to think about it, all it takes is one tiny spark of light to dispel vast arrays of darkness. Light always wins.

We have a hog farm, and our barns have pens with gates. If we ever accidentally leave a gate open, we open the barn door to find some chaos erupting inside because the pigs now have access to places they don't belong. In John 10, Jesus tells us that He is the gate and that whoever enters through Him will be saved. Like those pigs, we have wandered into places we never belonged, and we need a Savior to put us back under His care and provision inside the pen where we can find life to the full.

In that same passage, Jesus goes on to promise to be a Good Shepherd who lays down his life for the sheep. If you know anything about sheep, they are dumb, and it is no accident that God compares us to these dimwitted animals. We too are too dumb left on our own to make safe decisions, so we need a shepherd to guide us and to also protect us from the wolves who want to scatter and destroy.

In the 11th chapter of John, Lazarus, one of Jesus's closest friends, has died. When Jesus finally arrives on the scene, he comforts the sister by reminding her that, "I am the resurrection and the life. The one who believes in me will live, even though they die; and whoever lives by believing in me will never die. Do you believe this?" (John 11: 25, NIV). Do you get it? Do you feel it? Do you really know this? Jesus's entire purpose for coming here to this earth was so that you could have life. So, if you are feeling less than alive, maybe it is high time you become the child of the Most High King.

Sometimes life seems full of difficult decisions. Sometimes life seems full of opinions, making it beyond difficult to discern truths from lies. Sometimes life seems full of sickness and disease. But sometimes, I stop amid this fallen world and know deep within my soul that Jesus, my Savior and friend, really meant it when He promised to be The Way, The Truth, and The Life.

How, then, do I find this life to the full? I go to Him, remain in Him, bask in His presence as the only one who can give me life. When John 15:5 (NIV) says, "I am the vine; you are the branches. If you remain in me and I in you, you will bear much fruit; apart from me you can do nothing," I know too often how true this is, because when I set out on my own accord to live life without Him, I soon wither away with weariness. But when I stay connected to Him, I see abundant fruit.

Traditionally, these are the 7 "I Am" statements offered by Jesus while He did ministry here on earth. Scholars suggest an 8th that deserves our attention. If we go back to John 8:58 (NIV), Jesus says, "Very truly I tell you, before Abraham was born, I Am!" This would have been immediately recognized in his culture as a direct reference to Exodus 3:14 (NIV) where God tells Moses His name. God says, "I AM Who I AM. This is what you are to say to the Israelites: "I AM has sent me to you." Do you see it? The Great I Am sent His own I Am so that you would know whose you are.

Dearest friend, knowing Jesus is a double blessing for our lives. Understanding the evidence of his life story proves beyond a shadow of a doubt that our faith narrative is The Truth, and understanding how the story of Jesus can bring a brand-new plotline to your own story will prove beyond a shadow of a doubt that He really is worth living for.

Reflection Questions:

1. How does Jesus's life prove Christianity is reliable and real?
2. Which "I Am" statement speaks the most to you? Why?
3. How do you know that Jesus loves you?

Meet Me Here

~E-motions~

The lucky ones have cups that overfloweth.

When she sees those around her, their inner lives are always pouring out abundantly with the inner purity they permeate, even if they really aren't "good." You could call it a rewarding attribute of her character-to always see the positive, to always see the good in others.

But the measurement applies one direction only, and her own self-abased ruler stacks tall while she falls short.

So she compensates. I mean, that is helpful, right.

If she works harder, she will feel better.

If she works longer, she can measure up.

If she just keeps going and keeps pushing herself and refuses to settle and refuses to stop for even a second and ifshejustkeepsgoing andgoingandgoingandneverstops pushingandneverstopsdrivingherself harderandharderandhardershejustmay

Make it.

Make it or break it, right.

She often feels broken.

The outward spinning wheels of good deeds never end while the inward spinning web of lies convinces her to just keep keeping and maybe one day amid all her spiraling downward she will finally just...

Stop.

Stop pushing herself so hard. Stop hiding behind the masquerade of being just fine when she is only halfway close to kinda fine, and only even that kinda fine if she is in perpetual motion. Because she knows a silent stillness pervades peace, and so her addiction to disastrous motion refutes any allowance of apathy.

Movement masquerades madness.

It is her story she veils because she never slows down enough for anyone to read between her lines.

In between her lines are tear-stained mascara blots of pain she refuses to recognize.

She swirls across her dance floor of life painting flowers for Algernon with the feet of grace offered to everyone but herself, until He comes in.

Can He sweep her off her feet so she will finally slow to a halt and just be?

Just be enough. No need to run the ragged race of destitute denial.

Breathe.

Slow down.

Let Him in.

FOUR

THE SPIRIT OF FIRE

Anticipation Questions:

1. Characterize the Holy Spirit.
2. Why does the church have such different views/emphasis on the Holy Spirit?
3. Have you ever had an undeniable Holy Spirit encounter? If so, what was it like?

I grew up in a church that neglected to teach much about the Holy Spirit. I always knew He was part of the trinity, but it always seemed like no one wanted to tackle his role because we may be accused of being charismatic or weird or maybe too into the unexplainable supernatural.

Just on a side note before I go any further, the Holy Spirit is supernatural, but so are God and Jesus...It frustrates me that we somehow think avoiding the supernatural will make us seem more credible in the world's eyes. All the while, we refuse to offer any intellectual evidence for our beliefs. Instead, we tell people that we just need to have faith that what we believe in is real. Maybe if we would take the time to really study the defense of our faith and become solid in our apologetics and then share that hard evidence with non-believers, people would listen more and the whole supernatural vibe wouldn't seem absurd after all. The truth is, it is not absurd at all. Ghosts, or rather a ghost is real; He's my best friend.

In my upbringing, thinking about the Holy Spirit seemed a little bit on the side of loco, so no one really addressed Him. It was as if we thought we could insist on the Trinity while excluding one third of the equation. As I have started studying the Holy Spirit in the last few years, I have come to realize more and more that He really is such a vital part to any faith journey, and it is high time we talk about Him.

Understanding the role of the Holy Spirit does not necessitate a deep theological debate about the speaking of tongues. Obviously, this is an issue that arises in the Bible, and obviously entire books exist about what scripture teaches. Some denominations even believe that you have no proof of the Holy Spirit in you until you have spoken in tongues because that is the initial evidence of the infilling of God's Spirit in us. I have friends who speak in tongues, and I will be the last to say they are wrong for doing so because I simply don't know what they experience. I also know that I have never personally spoken in tongues, but beyond a shadow of a doubt, I have experienced very real Holy Spirit moments in my own life. Did speaking in tongues happen in some form during Pentecost? Absolutely because Acts tell us all about it. Is speaking in tongues a spiritual gift? Absolutely because 1 Corinthians discusses it. Am I going to hell if I never speak in tongues? That is not my interpretation of the scriptures as I study them, and from my own personal experiences with God working in my life, I can say beyond a shadow of a doubt that God is real, and His Spirit is alive in me.

If we refuse to consider the Holy Spirit beyond this idea of speaking in tongues, I fear we are missing a vital piece to our stories that should be rooted in Christ. A dear friend was once told by someone visiting the United States that foreign Christians are amazed at how much we American Christians can accomplish without the power of the Holy Spirit. I think this harsh statement holds a lot of validity; we work hard here in America mainstream churches to lead Christian lives all while skirting around an inclusion of the Holy Spirit because we don't understand Him. I also think it is high time we take the time to consider Him so we can do imaginably more than we can fathom for the sake of the kingdom.

So, what can we know about Him? Foremost, Jesus himself says He must leave so that He can send the Holy Spirit in His place because it is only then that we will be able to "do even greater things than these" (John 14:12, NIV). In John 14, Jesus outlines the plan; He must go to the Father so that He can then send the Holy Spirit who will be with us forever (v. 16, NIV). Jesus goes on to say, "The Counselor, the Holy Spirit, whom the Father will send in my name, will teach you all things and will remind you of everything I have said to you. Peace I leave with you; my peace I give you. I do not give to you as the world gives. Do not let your hearts be troubled and do not be afraid" (v. 26-27, NIV).

That passage is not scary and offers very tangible evidence of the role of the Holy Spirit. First, having the Holy Spirit in us is even more powerful than having Jesus walk beside us because God wants us to have His Very Spirit in us. Romans talks about how we are constantly in a battle between our spirit and our flesh. As Christians, we have a new spirit, the Spirit of Christ himself living in us. Do you see that? Feel that? Get that? THE VERY SAME POWER THAT ROSE JESUS FROM THE DEAD LIVES IN YOU! It doesn't get any better than that! Is that weird and supernatural? You bet. But it doesn't mean we necessarily walk around behaving in ways that others cannot interpret. It does mean that we walk around behaving in ways that are not natural.

I will give an example. As a teacher, I encountered students who did not want to partake in the educational environment. By the power of the Holy Spirit in me, I really could look at them with full love and acceptance even as they cussed me out. Could the other students interpret what I was doing on a basic level? Absolutely. Could they always understand how I could be so kind? Probably not, and it was especially a foreign concept to them if they had never encountered Christ's love. I could give another example. Someone largely wrongs me in a very deep and hurtful way and takes no responsibility for that wrong. Through the power of the Holy Spirit, I really can forgive them. Just ask Corrie ten Boom about her own experience with the

Nazi guard who was responsible for her sister's death in a concentration camp. Can we interpret the surface actions of someone living in the Holy Spirit? Yes. Is it the natural reaction? Well, that depends. It is completely unnatural when we are living by our own accord, in our flesh, but it is perfectly natural, or rather perfectly supernatural, when we are living by the Spirit.

The next thing this scripture demonstrates about the Holy Spirit is that He will teach us all things and remind us of the things Jesus says. 1 Corinthians 2 expounds on this, saying:

> "We have not received the spirit of the world but the Spirit who is from God, that we may understand what God has freely given us. This is what we speak, not in words taught us by human wisdom but in words taught by the Spirit expressing spiritual truths in spiritual words. The man without the Spirit does not accept the things that come from the Spirit of God, for they are foolishness to him, and he cannot understand them, because they are spiritually discerned. The spiritual man makes judgment about all things, but he himself is not subject to any man's judgment: For who has known the mind of the Lord that he may instruct him? But we have the mind of Christ" (v. 12-16, NIV).

Because Jesus left and sent the Holy Spirit, we have access to a deeper understanding of the realities we see around us. Think of it like an internal teacher who really can teach you all things and consistently fill your thoughts with the thoughts of God. Why then, do we sometimes experience quite the opposite, allowing destructive thoughts into our minds? Remember Romans 8? A battle between flesh and spirit? When you choose for your mind to dwell on the things of Christ and submit all thoughts to the power of the Holy Spirit, your thoughts align with biblical truths. When you choose to dwell on the things of the flesh, you just let Satan have a seat at your table; He loves nothing more than to fill you with lies.

God's very Spirit indwells in believers, and He desires to fill them with His ways and consistently remind them of all Jesus says. Yet we too often squelch the Holy Spirit. In the ESV, I Thessalonians 5:12 says, "Do not quench the Spirit." The NIV says, "Do not put out the Spirit's fire." When we ignore the Spirit of God who lives in us, we cease to be a fire that burns bright for Him.

I was preparing a lesson for a bible study one week, and beyond a shadow of a doubt, God gave me some teaching that has rocked my understanding of the Holy Spirit's power in me. It began with a reading in Matthew, and I stumbled across a phrasing that I had probably read countless times throughout my life. For some reason, on this day, it jumped out on the page (in case you haven't made the connection, that was a Holy Spirit moment with Him teaching me just like we talked about in the paragraphs above). So, I kept reading and thinking and reading and thinking. In chapter three, Matthew is telling about John the Baptist. He comes to the part in the story where the Pharisees and Sadducees approach John, and John unleashes some pretty heavy words, calling them a brood of vipers. He goes on to say, "After me will come one who is more powerful than I, whose sandals I am not fit to carry. He will baptize you with the Holy Spirit and with fire" (v. 11, NIV) Now, like I said, I had read that verse countless times before, but for some reason, the "and with fire" really stood out to me.

I have been taught all my life that baptism means we receive the gift of the Holy Spirit, but no one ever told me that Jesus' baptism also entailed fire. What did that even mean? As an English teacher who loves symbols, I found water and fire were always two of my favorite analogies to dissect in any piece of literature because they carry so much deeper meaning, and here, for the very first time, I was seeing fire associated with baptism. Was this an allusion to the refining power of fire? Was this a symbol of God's power coming to rest on us in the form of a flame that signified the speaking of tongues like the first church in Acts? On that day as I was reading, I believe God was saying these all certainly applied, but He wanted me to see something else.

God wanted me to see that when I accept Him, I receive the Fire of the Holy Spirit.

For years now, our family ventures west every summer to volunteer at a children's home that has now become our second home. Having grown up in southern Illinois, the only fear of fire we had were housefires or field fires; even these were not terrifying because a quick call to the local fire department meant all would soon be extinguished. Even as we lost our home to a fire three days before our first wedding anniversary, we did not live in fear of fire.

But then we established a second home in Montana where forest fires abound.

Forest fires ignite a much different reaction than fires in southern Illinois. Intense, unpredictable, life-threatening, they wreak havoc every summer on our western friends, and we soon came to appreciate the power of fire.

What if we looked at the power of a wildfire and applied that to the power of the Holy Spirit's fire promised to all believers?

Wildfires are all-encompassing. They are all-consuming, changing entire landscapes. They come across a place and burn out all the old so that new can grow. Asking the Holy Spirit to dwell in us should do this very same thing in us. He should consume us and change everything about us. He should be allowed access into all spaces of our lives, encompassing all areas, even the ones we hesitate to give up because of the comforts of strongholds even as they are destructive to us. He should be able to come in and refine us, burning away all the old so that the new can grow, a new that lives and breathes with an eternal perspective.

Wildfires need a dry and barren land to fully ignite. Southern Illinois receives too much moisture in a summer to ever be fully threatened by a wildfire, but out west, where the moisture is sparser, wildfires are a constant threat. Sometimes I think Americans need to lose access to comforts and be forced to live sparser lives so that the power of God can more easily move over us and fully ignite. It is when we finally come to the place where we are dry and barren and recognize our desperate need for living water that we become transformed and submit our lives to Christ. Maybe we should stop praying for struggles to go away. Too often, we ask God to take away the fire when what He really wants is to be invited to stand with us in the fire. It is then, in the heat of intense fire, that we experience Him on a much different level and come to know the true power of Him who lives in us.

Wildfires enact a chemical reaction, not just a physical change. I am not a scientist; it was my worst subject. But I do know there is a difference. A chemical change is irreversible. A physical change just changes the size and shape of the subject, but a chemical change is when a substance combines with another substance to create a brand-new substance. As Christians, we can repent of our sins and be baptized into a new life and start to change the way our life looks. We can change the size and shape of our lives and start to move in the right direction, but do you notice the key subject in all of that is "we." We can certainly enact a physical change in our lives, but it is only by the power of God's Spirit that we get a chemical reaction because chemical reactions demand TWO substances combining to form something new. Holy Spirit + you = You on fire, burning bright for God's kingdom.

Wildfires are wild. I know that seems like a dumb statement, but God himself calls us sheep, so you know, if the shoe fits...Too often, we say we want God in our lives but then we live normal lives. In fact, too often, people might not even know we are Christians; they could easily think we are just good, moral citizens. If our lives are ignited with the flame of God living in us, we will stand out. People WILL notice something different about us. Wildfires by their very nature are so big that it is hard for firefighters to control them. This world would love nothing more than to extinguish God's influence, and sadly enough, they are succeeding way more than they should. But, if we truly lived like wildfires, they would not be able to stop us. And in other countries we see this. The fastest growing Christian communities are in countries who face the fiercest persecution.

Wildfires emit such intense heat that they burn ahead of themselves and change the landscape well before actual contact. If I am impacting a young woman who is then going into her college community and impacting the people she meets, I am burning ahead of myself. If I am emitting such intense heat to be able to reach beyond my own personal contact, then I am also probably making the people in my midst rather uncomfortable. Have you ever tried to stand near a blazing fire? Your initial reaction is to get away because the heat hurts. Maybe if we lived a life on fire for God, others around us would feel the heat, experience conviction, and want to change direction too.

The more I studied Matthew 3, the more I realized that I had been missing something for way too long. John tells us clearly that Jesus will baptize us with the Spirit AND with fire. In Acts, God places a flame as a symbol of the power He is granting. And yet we Christians here in America have lived mediocre lives, singing songs like "This Little Light of Mine." Do I think we need to ban that song from our children's programs? Well, actually, maybe. God NEVER intended you to shine a little light; God intended you to BURN BRIGHT. Be a wildfire that no one could extinguish. If your light can be put out by hiding it under a little bushel, maybe the problem lies not with the power of the world around you, but with the lack of power, His power, within yourself. You were never meant to be just a little light.

Let's revisit the end of our John 14 passage. After Jesus says that the Spirit will be with us forever, that we will do even greater things than Jesus did by this power, that the Spirit will teach us all things and remind us of everything Jesus has spoken into us, He goes on to immediately say, "Peace I leave with you; my peace I give you. I do not give to you as the world gives. Do not let your hearts be troubled and do not be afraid" (v. 27, NIV). It is no coincidence that unleashing the power of the Holy Spirit leads directly to peace. After this comparison to wildfires, we can possibly more readily see how we don't need to be troubled or afraid because we have some stuff going on in us that is more powerful than we ever imagined. But if we are emitting intense heat to our neighbors and burning bright, bright enough to blind them, won't that bring more unrest and less peace? Most likely yes. But God also says that in this world we will have trouble, but we can take heart because HE has overcome the world. Peace never lies with the fleshly lives we live out as we exist here on earth; peace only lies with the eternal perspective of our Spirit-led, supernatural, this earth is not our home perspective. And that truly is a peace that passes all understanding, unless of course you have the very mind of Christ.

So how can you know if you have the Spirit in you? Galatians offers foundational truths, spelling out evidence of God's spirit in us. Are you a joyful person? Do you find peace even amongst intense struggles? Are you patient? Kind? Gentle? Do you live a life of goodness bestowed on others? Are you faithful even when it is hard? Do you have self-control? Most importantly, do you love...God's way? Oh, we can say we love, especially since our world has diluted that word to almost nothing, but true love is this, that He lays down his life for his friends. Is your love sacrificial? Do you think of others before you think of yourself? Do you see others the way God sees them? Do you live out love out loud?

I am far from perfect, but I do see evidence. A dear friend once gave a great analogy. He asked us to think about a fruit tree, and then reminded us that a fruit tree can only bear its natural fruit, and you cannot put cherries on an apple tree and honestly say the tree produced the cherry. Nor can you take someone who does not have the Holy Spirit and put these fruits on them and claim they naturally flow from the tree. A person who has the fire of the Holy Spirit within will naturally produce the fruits of the Holy Spirit: love, joy, peace, patience, kindness, goodness, gentleness, faithfulness, and self-control.

As I reflect on evidence of the Holy Spirit's presence in human beings like me and you, I can think of these two tests: fruits and encounters. Do you have the fruits listed above? Are they a natural outflowing because of the Spirit's presence in you? And do you have moments in your life of undeniable Spirit influence?

In my younger years, I was a nominal Christian with minimal Spirit influence. To be blunt, if you had met me in my later high school years and early college years, you likely would have laughed at the idea of me claiming Christ. I was a hot mess. Boys were my flaw, and I was far from Godly in my relationships with them. Most of this came as a result of my high school sweetheart crushing my heart; my natural reaction was to use and abuse.

I spent a semester at Oxford, and without knowing it, God was resetting me. For many years now, I can look back on that time in my life and see repeatedly how God was setting me on a better path, a path for him and not for me.

When I got home, I started fasting weekly, begging God to show me the man He had for me. During that time, he brought me to my husband Daniel. Then began the life of me pursuing God intentionally, and once I encountered the Holy Spirit in undeniably supernatural ways, I began to crave them more and more.

One story I would like to share to further exemplify the ways the Spirit works in our daily lives involves that high school sweetheart who stole my heart and then handed it back rather broken. In ways only God would conjure, He recently brought this boy now man into my sphere of influence through my church. Eugene and his wife not only started attending our church, but Eugene also began to develop a close friendship with Daniel, my husband. Want to talk about weird…I began praying for God to help me not be awkward around him because I certainly wanted him to develop a saving relationship with my Abba Father.

It was a Wednesday before Thanksgiving Day. I had worked all day at MCHS and had written about Eugene in Creative Writing when I gave everyone the assignment to free write about a person in our lives who brought pain. As I was driving home, my thoughts had no reason to travel back to him because I was fully focused on my grocery list of items needed for food preparations that evening and for the next morning. Very randomly, Eugene came into my mind and very surprisingly, I immediately asked God to give me a chance to encounter him and not be weird about it. Now, if you knew what every interaction had been for time on end leading up to that, you would know that the very LAST thing I would have willingly asked was to encounter him. It was all I could do to not run away at church.

My mind travels into other areas (if you know me, you know my mind is all over the place) and I think no more of that snippet of a moment in the vehicle. I stop at the grocery store and am headed to the aisle I need when out of the corner of my eye, I see Eugene. I stop in my tracks (luckily, I was walking quickly and had moved past his aisle already). I know God is speaking directly to me, ordaining this moment for me. So, I turn, have a pleasant but short conversation about Thanksgiving meals and kids, before grabbing my groceries and leaving. As I got into my vehicle, I knew that God was healing a very old wound in ways bigger than I could see.

God did that just for me. He asked me to present my requests to Him so He could then provide for them in ways I never dreamed. This is not the first time He has done such a thing for me, and I pray that as long as I live here on earth, He keeps showing up.

I pray the same for you. I pray that you have the fruits of the Holy Spirit flowing from your life and that you have regular supernatural encounters with Him as well. And I pray you never give up begging God to show up.

Reflection Questions:

1. How hot is your fire?
2. Why do we quelch the power of the Holy Spirit?
3. What is your Holy Spirit evidence?

Meet Me Here

-Moving Mountains-

One more time, one last time.

Time ticks tediously into the winds of insanity. But all you really want is to hold it somehow still in your hands just long enough to feel it, to own it. But it slips. Oh, how it slips away and away and away and yet you hold it, waterfalling cascades dancing around you as you turn this way and that to just hold on.

Just hold on. You wonder why you even try. Yet you do. The very thought of addiction benumbs your soul and yet out of embers and ashes you peer, wishing desperately to grasp one wisp of yellowed shine. The dawn of a new day never knocks, or maybe it did, and you just didn't hear it.

Why are you addicted to the insanity of normal?

The demons of normality are beckoning to be your best ally. Grasp hold of their sickening web and then you can break free to live an enchanted life, to unshackle the slave of your thoughts, break free, just be.

But you sense you are less than enough. So just this one time, just this one moment, you shall reject the heart's earnest cry to move mountains and one more time, just this one more time, you shall remain. Stay the course, hold your head high, be who they want you to be, who they need you to be.

Being for them breaks who you are.

You need more.

You need heights unsoared and valleys unkempt and struggles more real and yet more ensnaring than you can handle all while He comes to the rescue. He always comes to the rescue. But the chains of being what they expect are more wretched yet.

Maybe it's time.

They can't control you anymore because . . .

Maybe it is time.

Time to fight the constraints and fly into the glorious realm as He calls you by name into a world full of freedom, a world full of Him.

And as you fly, know that those who fight and flight are dancing together on the face of their failures, and you can step in time with them all, join the dance, be alive together in Him.

For together is all you really need.

FIVE

UNITY OF THE TRINITY

Anticipation Questions:

1. How would you explain God's ability to be three in one?
2. Define unity.
3. Define community.

Note: In my own struggles with the concept of the Trinity, God needed to strip me of my insistence on the three in one so I could see them as three separate in one because He had a re-vision to show me about unity. In no ways do I present the following arguments as a scholar of the trinity concept (but highly encourage you to study the writings of people who are scholars), and please know we really do serve ONE God. I merely present the meanderings of my own intellectual pursuits so that maybe you too can see how very unified the Trinity stands as the epitome of how we too, if we are Christians, should strive endlessly for a unity like theirs.

Understanding the Holy Trinity possibly creates some of the most complicated discussions for new believers regardless of their age. I have been a Christian for over thirty years, and I think in many ways I am just now gaining a more accurate picture of what this theological concept really means and why understanding it matters so much. If it is crucial to our understanding of God, and I believe it is, then why doesn't God make it plain from the start?

Isaiah 55 (NIV) begins with a call from God to come to Him and find that He will provide what we really need, the things that are everlasting. By verse 6 and into verse 7, we see that we can find God if we seek Him, that we can forsake our evil ways and find pardon from Him. Then verse 8 and 9 hit us with a different tune.

> "For my thoughts are not your thoughts, neither are your ways my ways," declares the Lord. "As the heavens are higher than the earth, so are my ways higher than your ways and my thoughts than your thoughts."

Or is it really a different tune?

We often hear verse 8 and 9 in isolation anytime we come up against a concept that is difficult for our earthly minds to comprehend. Although it is certainly true that God's ways and thoughts are higher than our ways and thoughts, I am not certain that the context implies freedom for us to give up our attempts to understand Him.

In context of chapter 55, it seems that God reminds us that everything He does is way beyond our initial understanding, but even yet He is inviting us to come to Him and find that He will provide us with everlasting things which I believe includes everlasting truths. The passage goes on to make comparisons that demonstrate how God's word will not return to Him empty, "but will accomplish what I desire and achieve the purpose for which I sent it" (Isaiah 55:11, NIV). God intends to have even his creation display his renown for an everlasting sign, and we are invited to be part of that song. How do we do that? Remember the verse (1 Corinthians 2: 16) we talked about in chapter four where we see that, as Christians, we are offered the very mind of Christ? This verse reminds us that we come to be part of His song by coming to Him to begin to know his very mind.

If God's mind were simple, He would make all precepts plain and easy to understand. Although He certainly wants us to come to know Him, He also wants us to recognize the depths of Him as we do so which means many concepts take mental strength on our behalf and intense submission. When we combine aggressive study with earnest reliance on Him as our teacher, we find great truths that move our entire worlds into a whole new realm of understanding.

The concept of the Trinity is one of those things that requires relentless study in conjunction with steadfast submission for Him to reveal the truth of His nature.

For more years than I can count, I heard descriptions about the Trinity that I found necessary to question. All arguments derived from the Christian insistence that we serve only one God which sets us apart from so many other polytheistic religions. Let me be clear right now in saying I firmly assert Christianity as a monotheistic religion. We serve only one God. But the way I understand His three parts no longer fully aligns with many years of explanations I heard growing up in the church.

Have you ever heard someone describe the Trinity like the scientific understanding of water as a substance? Water can be in the form of water, the form of ice, or the form of vapor. People would tell me that God's Trinity is much like this. He can appear in the form of a Father, in the form of a Son, or in the form of a Spirit. A similar explanation was that just like I can be a mom and a daughter and a teacher yet still be the same person, so too can God be a Father and a Son and a Spirit and yet still be the same person.

I understand how simplifying this concept helps us to begin to wrap our minds around how we do indeed serve ONE God who exists in the form of three parts, but I think for too long I settled for the easy explanation that did very little to really show me what God wanted me to see all along and the beauty of how understanding his Trinity on a whole new level can change everything.

So, let me ask a question. What if God really does exist in three distinct persons? What if God is three very different beings yet those three really do exist as one because they are so unified that they can't help but have one "mind" and one "existence"?

I was on a mission trip this summer in Montana. I had asked a few dear friends to send me texted prayers throughout the week. From the onset of the trip, I felt some very real opposition from Satan and sensed that God wanted to move big, but Satan had roadblocks set up all along the way. I did not want to fall over those obstacles any more than I had to. I wanted God to be able to use me to His fullest intent, so I reached out for help. One morning as I was up early to finalize the devotion I would soon share with the group at the start of our day, I was praying, begging God to speak into me. The day before had been very hard, and the days ahead were about to get harder. I received a text message from my dear friend Jerri, and she shared things that my other dear friend Deborah had just shared the night before. Even more so, the verse she chose was the very verse associated with Pinehaven, the ranch where we were serving. She had no idea how the things she shared would especially impact me that morning, but God did. The Holy Spirit had given Jerri and Deborah the exact same encouragement and led them both to share with me within twelve hours of each other. You can call that coincidence; I call that Divine Unity.

The other day I texted three young friends, asking them to send encouraging messages to someone they were all connected with. I asked them some very specific things to speak into her. One of them texted me back privately right away and asked if I knew she had already texted our young friend. Although I knew she had sent a text, I had no idea what the text had said; it had said the exact same things I asked them to speak into her about. Again, you can call that coincidence; I call that Divine Unity.

Too often we have tried to minimize the Trinity into our understanding without any consideration for the supernatural ability to really be fully distinct and yet so fully in-tune with one another that they really do become one. This is unity at a whole new level, and I think it is a level God desperately wants to show us because it will change the way we do life at all levels.

Let's look at some scriptures to see if this distinction rings true. In Mark 1: 9-11, we see the story of Jesus' baptism. The scripture says, "As Jesus was coming up out of the water, he saw heaven being torn open and the Spirit descending on Him like a dove. And a voice came from heaven: 'You are my son, whom I love; with you I am well pleased'" (Mark 1:11, NIV). Do you see it? Three very distinct beings permeate this passage. Jesus is in the water, the Holy Spirit is in the dove, and the Father's voice presides over it all.

Matthew 28 gives us the great commission, and Jesus tells us to baptize others in the name of the Father, and of the Son, and of the Holy Spirit. In Luke, when the angel tells Mary she will birth Jesus, the angel says that the Holy Spirit will come on her and that the power of the Most High God will overshadow her. John 15 relates Jesus saying that the Holy Spirit will come because Jesus will send Him to us from God his father. In Paul's second letter to the church in Corinth, he ends with these words, "May the grace of the Lord Jesus Christ, and the love of God, and the fellowship of the Holy Spirit be with you all" (2 Corinthians 13:14, NIV). In all cases, each partner in the Trinity holds his own identity.

One more passage can assert further explanation. Paul writes the book of Romans as a guide to the Christians in Rome. One major struggle he addressed lay between the Jews and the Gentiles who alike were seeking to follow "The Way." Romans is meaty with numerous layers of theological concepts, but rich with applicable meaning for each of us. In chapter five, Paul reminds us that we are justified by faith, made right with God not of our own doings but through what Christ did on the cross. Because of this great gift, we can rejoice in the hope of the glory of God, AND we can rejoice in our sufferings. He tells us that, "suffering produces perseverance; perseverance, character; and character, hope. And hope does not disappoint us because God has poured out his love into our hearts by the Holy Spirit whom he has given us" (Romans 5:5, NIV). Paul then immediately reminds us that when we were powerless, Christ died for us, stating, "God demonstrates his own love for us in this: while we were still sinners, Christ died for us" (Romans 5:8, NIV).

God as the Father stands as the pillar of the Trinity. He pours out his love for us by sending the Son and by sending the Spirit. God the Father did not come to the earth as a human; He sent His Son. God the Father did not come to the earth at Pentecost; He sent His Spirit. But even yet, God came to the earth to be among us; that has been part of His story from the beginning. Even back to the Israelites wandering in the desert, God tabernacled among his people. The burning bush? Elijah's still, small whisper? Abraham and Isaac's provided sacrifice? Walking in the Garden of Eden? See, the list could go on and on and on of how much God has inhabited the earth. Don't forget that He is omnipresent, everywhere at all times. So, if God is everywhere at all times, is God the Father the only one who is everywhere at all times? That will hardly seem the case if we really do have only one God. Is the Holy Spirit also omnipresent? And what about Jesus? If they are fully God, and I believe they are, then they too would be omnipresent which means they have no need to be three distinct persons. All parts of God exist in all places at all times so can't they just be One with no distinction? Or does God have something even bigger than that in mind as He begins to reveal His very triune nature to us?

Let's take a sidestep for a moment to observe something Jesus indicates to us numerous times throughout his time here on earth. John 5:19-23 (NIV) says:

> "Jesus gave them this answer, 'I tell you the truth, the Son can do nothing by himself; he can do only what he sees his Father doing, because whatever the Father does the Son also does. For the Father loves the Son and shows him all he does. Yes, to your amazement he will show him even greater things than these. For just as the Father raises the dead and gives them life, even so the Son gives life to whom he is pleased to give it. Moreover, the Father judges no one, but has entrusted all judgment to the Son, that all may honor the Son just as they honor the Father. He who does not honor the Son does not honor the Father who sent him'."

Clearly, Jesus sees himself as someone distinct from the Father, yet also as someone acting fully in unity with God. God has given over judgment to Jesus and yet they are working so much as a team that it becomes impossible to distinguish one from the other. This is just one example of countless times Jesus refers to God as His "authority" with Jesus acting fully in accordance with what God designates. Yet at the same time, we see that Jesus has full authority in himself as well since He is equally divine; he lives, however, in submission to His Father.

I am not a scholar. I hold no claims on the level of intelligence that numerous philosophers present. But I do think God wants me to see something about his Triune nature that moves beyond just a classification of water, ice, and vapor. And I think He wants the same for you.

If God exists simply as just one with different "hats" to wear as needed in various moments, we miss out on two very important blessings: community and unity.

In Genesis 1:1, we meet a plural God in the word Elohim. God already exists in three distinct persons who all operate so jointly that they really are one. From the beginning, God values relationships. He values community so much that even his own nature has three distinct parts. Could the God of the universe exist as one God with only one part? You bet. But that is not who He is, and that is not who He wants us to be either.

Could you and I exist as one person with only one part? You bet. But life will be lonely and miserable and then you will die and go to hell and live the rest of your eternity in complete isolation. It is no wonder that the cruelest torture used is isolation. It deprives us of the very intimacy God instilled in us because He made us in His image, an image of three persons in One.

So, understanding the Trinity on this level becomes an invitation for you to also exist as an entity beyond yourself. You were designed for more than just you; you were designed to be in relation with God (the triune God) and with others which creates its own trinity of sorts: God, you, others. Even the greatest commandment reminds us that we are to love God and love others. You were made to exist in God's special Trinity established for his people, living in complete unity with Him and others to the point where all distinctions fade, and it becomes impossible to see the varying wills. We were made to be so tuned in to one mission that we become one huge force, fully aligned on a single perspective, seeing life through the eyes of God.

Have you noticed that I said two blessings but seem to have somehow meshed them into one? You cannot have community without unity, and you will automatically have community once you have unity. The English language in particular sets this up inherently in the very language.

Break down the word community into two parts and see what you get: common unity.

When we live so much in step with God and his ways, we will be fully united in Christ. When we live fully united in Christ, we will find ourselves amid a community richer than we could ever imagine.

A year ago, we had a reunion of sorts with various friends we met through Pinehaven. Our friend James had flown in from Oregon for a few weeks, and one Saturday, other friends drove in to share the day together. Every time I think back on that day, I feel overwhelming blessings. I can still sense the indescribable feeling of simply belonging in that moment. Nothing this world has to offer mattered to any of us; we simply wanted to just be together and share the love of God with one another.

As James departed, we were all homesick, even though we never left our earthly home. With his visit, we had tasted a deeper glimpse of heaven where we simply get to be united under Christ. Weeks later, we got a letter in the mail from James. He wrote, "While I had a blast eating and hunting, the fellowship that we shared was my favorite part. The more I travel and visit Christians, the more Paul's letters come to life. Sometimes I am tempted to think that heaven may be boring. However, I am quickly reminded that this is a lie. If fellowship in the name of Jesus (on earth) is rewarding, how much greater fellowship will be in the presence of our Savior."

While James was with us, he asked me one day to think about my perfect day. The question came after our Saturday reunion, and immediately, with tears in my eyes, I saw that Saturday unfold before me anew.

I wish I could somehow amass the right words to describe that feeling, a day where all is well, and you are surrounded by Godly people. Pure love is the only word that attempts to paint an adequate portrait of all the joy swirling yet settling. But I could not muster anything worthy of describing that day; nothing sufficiently relates the beauty that God offers to us. Better yet, I know that an even greater day awaits me on the other side of this life here, and I hope to see you there too.

That, my friends, is why it is vital for us to understand the depths of God's triune nature. Through his very makeup, he invites us to something deeper, something richer, something fuller than a life lived on our own. He invites us to live in common unity, to live in community, to live out a life loving Him, loving others, and serving both as we daily grow one step closer to the full unity we will experience once we really do get to go home.

Philippians 2: 1-11 (NIV): "If you have any encouragement from being united in Christ, if any comfort from his love, if any fellowship with the Spirit, if any tenderness and compassion, then make my joy complete by being like-minded, having the same love being one in spirit and purpose. Do nothing out of selfish ambition or vain conceit, but in humility consider others better than yourselves. Each of you should look not only to your own interests, but also to the interests of others. Your attitude should be the same as that of Christ Jesus.

> Who, being in very nature God, did not consider equality with God something to be grasped, but made himself nothing, taking the very nature of a servant, being made in human likeness. And being found in appearance as a man, he humbled himself and became obedient to death-even death on a cross! Therefore, God exalted him to the highest place and gave him the name that is above every name, that at the name of Jesus every knee should bow, in heaven and on earth and under the earth, and every tongue confess that Jesus Christ is Lord, to the glory of God the Father."

Want to truly live? Then ask yourself daily how to be more like Jesus, invite the Holy Spirit to take over and empower you to be something more than you could ever be on your own, and sit down at the feet of your Father to do only and always what He wills. Submission of our own wills may be the hardest thing we ever do, but it is the one thing we must do if we are ever to feel like we are loved and that we belong.

Common unity has become rather uncommon. Maybe it's time to revive unity for the sake of community.

Reflection Questions:

1. Describe a time where you experienced true community.
2. Why does God need to be three in one?
3. Why does God's church in America lack unity?

Meet Me Here

-It's Written in the Sand-

She sees it clearly, crystal glimmering through smoky haze.

It looks like trailing lines webbing into a larger pattern in the sand. At first, as she watched it unfold, the lines seemed haphazard, then messy. For a long time, they just seemed broken, but now that time has etched its way into her perspective, she is starting to see the beauty of it all.

She really is more beautiful than she knows.

The first lines ebbed and flowed through her childhood innocence with no real pattern. A zig zag here, a curve there, but as puberty hit, they became very awkward. I mean, it was junior high after all. She thought by then that she knew Him, but she was kidding herself. We often kid ourselves into our false realities that leave us sinking in quicksand.

The scars of choices' unforeseen consequences left her in pieces, cracked mosaic of seeping sands. In those years, she felt He left her.

He never left.

He was always there. He was there before she became life in her mother's womb, and He was there when she was conceived. He was there when she breathed her first, and He was there when she learned to take a step. He was there when she braved the doors of an education, and He was there when she graduated.

He was there for every unimportant miniscule happening in her life, and He was there for every monumental milestone. He was there for every tear, and for every joy.

He was always there.

She couldn't see it for so long. Eyes choose to see light or dwell in the dimmed phantom shadows. She was a night dweller for some time. When the first light peeped through, she hid her eyes in shame.

How could He come to me? How could He look at me?

How could He love me?

He loves her; oh, how He loves her.

Jesus loves her, this I know; I see His footprints in the sand.

SIX

YES, THAT'S THE BOOK FOR ME

Anticipation Questions:

1. What's in the Bible?
2. Why is the Bible important?
3. How would you describe your relationship with God's word?

If I am living life the way I should as a Christian, God is my best mentor, Jesus is my best friend, the Holy Spirit is my best choice, and the Bible is my best read...or is there something even more?

Did you know that the Bible is likely the book with the most copies in circulation but one of the least read books? Something is obviously wrong with this picture.

Maybe you are like me, and you grew up hearing stories from the Bible. I have always loved a good story (probably a good indicator for why I have a Master of Arts in English), and the Bible stories I heard growing up were some of my favorites. Who doesn't love a story about a boat with cute animals? Or the adventures of a missionary? An intense show of power and then a still small voice? A young shepherd boy and his giant? The parting of a massive sea?

The main storylines seemed to always tie back to another story, the one that we all were supposed to make sure we got. It was the story of a man named Jesus who was born to a virgin Mary, grew up as God's son and became a great teacher, eventually led a wild ministry for about three years, and then he died on a cross, rose on the third day, appeared to hundreds, and then went to hang out with his Dad.

It truly is a great story. Trust me, I know. As an English major, I have studied the elements of literature for more hours than I care to mention, and this Jesus story...well, it really does have it all going on.

But what would happen if we never read anything more than the familiar stories we heard as a child? Or maybe you didn't grow up hearing these stories, so you have no idea what I am talking about. Perhaps you fall somewhere in the middle of this line where you know a story here and there, but they are scattered pieces of plots. Regardless, the first problem for most Christians is they don't read God's word to study it. It is not their best read; as a matter of fact, it doesn't even make their top ten.

What if I craved the Bible so much that I was like Ezekiel who eats it? Ok, well that is actually a bad analogy taken out of context (which is a bad habit to have when reading your Bible, just so you know), but hopefully you get the point. Do I crave God's word more than the very air I breathe?

Perhaps the Bible should for sure be my best read, the one thing I consume daily and cannot imagine going a day without it, but what if it was even more than that? What if it served as the compass for my entire life?

Flannery O'Connor once said, "Truth does not change by our ability to stomach it emotionally." I have read a lot of O'Connor in my studies, and almost every story includes some grotesque surprise, so it no wonder she wrote this, but I also have studied her personal life and know that she writes with the intent to hopefully shock the reader into seeing their own depravity in a character who seems good on the surface. So, she creates stories that can be hard for us to stomach in attempts to shock us into seeing our own false natures so we will be willing to submit to Christ. In case you are wondering, I would absolutely recommend reading a story or two of hers... In the meantime, think about how our inability to stomach something does not alter the fact that it still may be true of our human nature. Is it harder to stomach the fact that many Christians, maybe even you, don't actually read their Bible, or the fact that the things said in it are the absolute truth, so you better get busy reading and applying it?

I have been teaching my high school students' various concepts from a book called *Understanding the Faith* by Jeff Myers who is one of the major leaders of Summit Ministries. And I have learned a lot about the Bible that I would love to share with you in condensed form in the pages to come.[7]

The Bible stands as The Source of Truth. Notice the capitalizations. This very book you are currently reading is far from Truth with a capital T, even as I hope to point to capital T truths. I am a flawed human being, and although I certainly hope I am influenced by the Holy Spirit even as I type these very words, I also do not have the audacity to place myself in the same position as the Biblical authors. God called them for a special commission: to write His Word for countless generations to come. The Bible alone is our guiding Truth.

2 Timothy 2:15 (NIV) says, "Do your best to present yourself to God as one approved, a workman who does not need to be ashamed and who correctly handles the word of Truth." Paul is reminding Timothy that we are uniquely called to study God's word and handle it correctly. How do we handle it correctly? First, we need to understand its purpose. Jeff Meyers writes, "The Bible...is not even primarily about us at all. It is about God and what He has done, is doing, and will do in the world and for all eternity. It is from God and for humans." He goes on to say that the Bible is a compass. It is not meant to be seen just as a list of dos and don'ts; it is not meant to just be stories of people so we can better understand how to behave; it is not meant to just spell out the steps of salvation. Instead, the Bible is about God, his special revelation to us of who He is, what he values, and how He loves.[8]

Let's take a quick moment to talk about that word revelation. I have often heard Christians saying that they are asking God for

[7-8] Myers, Jeff. *Understanding the Faith: A Survey of Christian Apologetics.* Summit Ministries, 2016.

direction in their lives and are seemingly frustrated with His lack of reply. Although I certainly believe God acts according to His time and not mine, I also believe we can throw up little prayers when we want an answer and forget that God offers us revelation. He offers general revelation through his creation so that none can claim exemption for lack of knowledge; Romans 1:20 reminds us that men are without excuse, meaning all mankind stands accountable regardless of their direct encounter with the Word of Truth. But God also offers special revelation through His Word. And you want to know something that may surprise you? The more you are in His word, the more you will receive revelations. Go figure, huh? But really, we often act surprised by a lack of revelation all while we refuse to crack open the surface of our dusty Bibles. Opening His Word will reveal endless Truths to us so we can better understand His will for our lives because we better understand Him.

Understanding God's character will take you farther in life than anything else. He is not just a watchmaker who started the world spinning and then left. Instead, He is immanent and transparent; He is God with us yet also set apart in holiness. God is eternal, omnipotent, omnipresent, omniscient, wise, righteous, loving, merciful, full of grace, just, three in one, self-existent, and the list goes on and on. As we already discussed Him, I hope you are already seeing more and more of just how very Big He is. And His word continues to be a source of Truth about his character and His great love for us.

Some may be having a bit of a rebuttal in the head by this point, asking a vital question. How can we know that the Bible is even a reliable source? Great question. Have you studied the authenticity of the Bible? If you haven't, I challenge you to do so because it will knock your socks off. More evidence exists for the historicity of the Bible as a text than absolutely any other ancient document we study in professional education. Even atheists cannot deny the archaeological evidence for the Bible documents.

After studying the validity of the texts, you will find that the Bible has forty authors written over the span of 1500 years, and they don't disagree with one another. You will certainly find different focal points for the same story because God asked humans to author his inspired word which means personalities always showed up in the writing, but the textual evidence aligns. With that many authors over that many years, surely something would have enabled the whole thing to be torn apart with little chance of rebuttal. But it didn't. And then, as we already talked about in chapter three, countless prophecies align as well, and the very person of Jesus fulfills every single one. When you combine the evidence of Jesus with the evidence of the Bible, you have a more solid case than any other worldview out there.

So, if we can study the Bible as a historical document objectively and discern full reliability, and if we can also say that the Bible is about God and not us, then how do we go about reading this thing so it can be the compass of our lives, pointing us to true direction?

Anytime I tackle a text for meaning, I find it helpful to understand the objective and the outline and use those two tools to help me piece together everything going on within the story. The Bible's objective is all that has already been mentioned, but I also think it is important to understand the Bible as a metanarrative, the story beyond a story. In this case, the Bible is God's story which goes beyond my story, your story, the story of every human being who ever lived minus Jesus Christ. When we understand that our individual life story is part of a bigger story, it helps bring clarity to our own pieces and clarifies meaning for you and me in our day to day lives.

I will give an example. When I understand that I am living under a story way bigger than mine, I can start to see purpose in pain. In high school, I made some dumb decisions which then led to a cycle of self-destruction for a few years. I finally stopped and asked God to speak Truth back into me which has undoubtedly led me to my current place of ministry. Without God's overarching narrative, I would have first never come out of my messiness and would have continued down a road of devastation. Perhaps more impactfully, however, is how I fully see every day how God's story of grace changed my entire life. Instead of being angry for the pain I felt for those years because of fractured relationships and misplaced affections, I can see how that very pain drove me into the arms of God to make me whole again in Him.

Understanding the Bible as a metanarrative helps me make sense of my own story, but it also helps me know how to study God's story, but as I said, I need the objective and the outline to work hand in hand for me to better find meaning from a text. What, then, is the outline of the Bible? Summit Curriculum does a really great job breaking down God's story into three big parts: Creation, Fall, and Redemption. The Redemption phase has numerous pieces within it. First, redemption is initiated through God's covenants with His people. Redemption becomes complicated when mankind continues to disobey God through the periods of kings, but prophets step in to predict a coming redemption through a messiah. Jesus comes to earth to fulfill those prophecies and accomplish redemption through kingdom restoration, and then He sends the Holy Spirit to flame the fire for the birth of the church which becomes redemption applied. And one day, the kingdom will come, and God's Will shall be done on earth as it is in Heaven, ushering in a new creation where redemption is completed. Oh, what a day that will be.

So where are we in this story? We are hanging out in the phase of Redemption Applied. Why does that matter? It reminds us of our job; if we are not applying the story of redemption to our own lives and leading others into the story as well, then no application is happening at all.

And so, we have circled back to the beginning problem of having 4.3 Bibles on average in American households while way more than the majority of Americans live with no applicable redemption playing out in their lives. Think about the very definition of redemption: the action of being saved or gaining possession of something in exchange for payment. I don't know about you, but when I look around, I see a whole lot of people who are far from saved. Merriam-Webster gives the following list of antonyms for saved: abandoned, desolate, forgotten, rejected, vacant, ignored, discarded, junked, waste. Too many relate too well, feeling very much forsaken in life. Maybe it is time to change that.

Let's say you are ready to make that change but are still unsure how to study your Bible. Jeff Meyers offers ten mistakes to avoid that may be helpful. Mistake 1-We assume that the Bible doesn't need to be interpreted. Mistake 2-We assume that that the Bible applies uniquely to us. Mistake 3-We ignore passages that don't fit our theology. Mistake 4-We treat the

Bible allegorically. Mistake 5-We feel that our study is fruitless if we have not discovered a new truth. Mistake 6-We focus on what the text "means to me." Mistake 7-We assume the Bible isn't relevant to us today. Mistake 8-We take the Bible out of context. Mistake 9-We interpret the Bible based on contemporary moral standards. Mistake 10-We try to make the Bible fit contemporary standards for political correctness.

He follows these ten mistakes with ten steps to reading the Bible well and truly. Step 1: Commit to reading the Bible and studying it. Step 2. Read the Bible in context. Step 3: Choose a translation. Step 4: Understand the genre. Step 5: Understand the context. Step 6: Understand the content. Step 7: Look for relationships. Step 8: Study words. Step 9: Bring your experiences to bear. Step 10: Courageously pursue a response.[9]

This is a lot to take in, and I would encourage you to read this section at the bare minimum of the book *Understanding the Faith* so you can understand what Jeff means by these mistakes and steps. But regardless, I hope you take just one step and then another and then another. Perhaps most importantly, don't go it alone. Find someone who will help you study and apply God's word.

Studying and applying the Bible changes everything. Why would I say studying and applying and not just reading? Well, I have known numerous people who know their Bible well, much like the Pharisees and Sadducees, but they do not live out a life that seems saved by grace. My dear friend, God invites you to let His word penetrate your very soul. Hebrews 4:12 says, "For the word of God is living and active. Sharper than any double-edged sword; it penetrates even to dividing soul and spirit, joints and marrow; it judges the thoughts and attitudes of the heart." Do you see how digging into God's word will change everything?

Fear of change may just be why the Bible is the most circulated publication but collects abundant dust. We want to know what God says, but we don't want to know what He says about us. We want to know God if it will give us a quick fix or even validation for our upright standing, but we don't want the parts that require change in us. But

---

9 Myers, Jeff. *Understanding the Faith: A Survey of Christian Apologetics*. Summit Ministries, 2016.

God is in the business of change. You know why? Because without a change, we can never become more like Him, and becoming more like Him is the best possible thing for us.

If you were a piece of chocolate, would you want to be a morsel fallen to the floor and then eaten by a mouse, or would you want to be part of a decadent chocolate mousse cake served to a king? Too often, we settle for the mouse's morsel when we were meant for royalty.

For years, I attended church, read my Bible, said some prayers, attended lots of church services, and spent some time serving in various ways. Then I met my friend Amy. We both had small children, so meeting at normal Bible studies was difficult. We started meeting late in the evening one day a week once the kids were in bed, and when we started meeting, I had no idea how Amy would change my life. You see, Amy taught me how to study my Bible; she showed me how to ingest it daily and let it penetrate every part of me. Amy let God use her to change my life.

Dear friend, I wish I could sit with you and be your Amy vessel. I am praying you have found your own Amy to do this book with so you too can be forever changed by a re-vision of what it really means to follow the God who made you and desperately wants a relationship with you. My Bible is not just my best read. My Bible is my lifeline every single step of the way through this life, and I hope you find it to be the same for you. I beg you...let God speak to you through His word and taste and see that He is oh so good. You really will never be the same.

Reflection Questions:

1. Choose one passage of scripture. Write it out word for word. Then write out what it means to you.
2. Share your passage and reflection (your answer to number 1) with a friend.
3. Commit to reading your Bible ten minutes a day for the next month.

Meet Me Here

-The Deaner Dis-ease-

I never went up to see her.

It had nothing to do with fear of the casket. I have seen my fair share of dead died young in cracked oak shells while we pretend to shelter their souls from the winds of hell.

It had more to do with the hard, cold fact that she had been dead to me long before.

I guess you could say I knew. I knew the moment they told me she was in a coma, and I would hold one of her dear friends through her own grief of regrettable loss.

I guess you could say it was the day I ran into her in the high school office, and her presence caught me off guard, forcing my feigned joy in seeing her.

I think maybe the better answer is the day she graduated and stopped coming to my room. The moments spent watching her slip away because the pieces of her shattered heart were too fragmented to hold onto as she kept littering them all over that high school.

Did she lose her heart that night during their one last hoorah, refusing to acknowledge it was the final straw for her beaten soul?

Or did she lose it after that in pieces as she gave herself away and away and away to anything to take the pain?

I honestly don't know. I was no longer in her confidant the moment she walked across that stage, and somehow even then I knew she was lost forever.

They say she died of a tumor. I know better.

She died of the same thing they are all dying of.

The casket was open. All I had to do was walk up and peek in. But something else held my gaze, or rather someones. Floods of heartache and students who knew her too well, knew me too well. And all I could do was sit there in dis-ease as I watched their souls dying rapidly throughout the room. And all the while I held the golden antidote, the shot if you will. But how can you grant reprieve to a room who refuses the truth of what you hold? It's like hell inside unfurling its harsh reality, and all I could do was weep and offer them their free will to choose their deaths; love like this hurts more than you can imagine. But He knows. He always knows.

The dis-ease of our dying youth is the shattered pieces of broken hearts. Pieces that can only be mended by One alone. And yet they go on dying, long before their time. The saddest Dis-ease of humankind.

SEVEN

TO BE OR NOT TO BE

Anticipation Questions:

1. What does it mean to be a Christian?
2. What has been your experience with "Christian" people? Helpers? Hurters? Etc.?
3. What should the life of a Christian look like?

"In Antioch, the disciples were first called Christians" (Acts 11:26).

I would venture that those who claim Christ, along with those who don't, all struggle to define what it means to be a Christian. For some, event attendance grants the title; for others, it requires something much different. For nonbelievers, it likely constitutes a claim to a certain life that never actually lives up to the namesake's expectations which is why they have personally deemed it unnecessary to make such a claim; who needs a name when life doesn't transform?

Claiming Christ should be transformative. The term Christian has a base word (Christ) with the -ian suffix which means from, related to, or like. Hence, people who claim this name are in essence saying, "I am from Christ, related to Him, and living like Him." A rather tall order it seems.

How is a Christian "from Christ"? Genesis 1:1 states that in the beginning was God and the original word for God there is Elohim which is a plural word. The Triune was present from the beginning; Christ was part of the creation. We derive our very existence from Him. 2 Corinthians 5:17 (NIV) says, "Therefore, if anyone is in Christ, he is a new creation; the old has gone, the new has come." Although everyone lives and moves and breathes because of God initiating creation, only those who have accepted Jesus as their savior and submitted their lives to Him can claim to be a Christian. Once that salvation happens, we gain a new identity as someone who is now from Christ.

Being a Christian also means we are related to Christ. God exists as the Father of Jesus, and when we become a "Christian," we too are children of God. John 1:12 (NIV) says, "Yet to all who received Him, to those who believed in His name, He gave the right to become children of God." Romans 8:14 (NIV) says, "Those who are led by the Spirit of God are sons of God." Galatians 3:26 (NIV) says, "You are all sons of God through faith in Christ Jesus."

Living like Him is likely the most difficult part. It is easy to accept the gift of salvation and receive our new identity that makes us from Christ and sons of God. But to become like Christ is on a whole different level of intensity. So, what does it actually look like to be a Christian?

First, let's understand the concept of how the name came to be to see if that helps us understand what it looks like. Scripture tells us that after Jesus died and rose again, he appeared to many. Then he ascends into Heaven to be with God, and his followers are not exactly fulfilling the Great Commission initially. Many reasons exist for the delay, but just know that Pentecost is when God sends His Spirit upon his people to begin the global mission of spreading "The Way." The local church explodes until Stephen is stoned, and then as the people scatter, God's truth is taken to the world. Meanwhile, Saul becomes Paul and Peter gets his commission to take the good news to the Gentiles (if you don't know the story about the large sheet and Cornelius, you should check it out in Acts 10 and 11). Then we pick up our story in Acts 11:19 (NIV): "Those who had been scattered by persecution with Stephen traveled as far as Phoenicia, Cyprus and Antioch, telling the message only to Jews. Some of them, however, men from Cyprus and Cyrene, went to Antioch and began to speak to Greeks also, telling them the good news about the Lord Jesus." As the church in Antioch grows, great numbers of people come to faith and are first called Christians there in Antioch.

Why Antioch? I am quite certain much research exists to delve deeply into this question, but I think for our purposes, one significant concept should strike us. Antioch is a place where both Jews and Greeks (Gentiles) are coming to know about "The Way." From the beginning, God's plan is for all nations, tongues, tribes to know Him personally, to know they can come from Him, be related to Him, and be like Him; you are personally invited to add the -ian to Christ. You see, it was in Antioch that they were first called Christians because God desperately wants to tell you that you are invited into the family.

But what does it look like to be a Christian other than everyone is invited? Does it mean I start going to church on Sundays? Does it mean I walk the aisle and get wet? Does it mean I start reading my Bible and praying? Does it mean I stop all my immoral habits?

James reminds us that faith without deeds is dead. Paul in his letter to the Corinth church emphasizes that our bodies are a temple of the Holy Spirit so we must honor God with our body. Transformed behavior certainly indicates behavioral change, but I fear too often that we claim Christ and allow the transformation to penetrate our actions only, refusing access to our hearts.

It should not surprise you that Jesus repeatedly sought the oppressed, the overlooked, the underprivileged. He chose to spend his time with the walked-on, beat-down, cast-out, smelly, poor, got-nothing-to-offer-and-think-I-have-no-worth "nobodies" for good reason: He knew their hearts were most open to letting Him make them a somebody.

Being a true Christian, someone who sincerely follows him and wants to be like Him, does not bode well with the popular or the status-ed. It is not an elite club for only those who can rise to the top of society as somebody. Christianity is for the orphaned, the widowed, the prostitute, the alien, the sinners of this world. Christianity is for everyone who is willing to submit to being like Him and taking on His identity.

I recently helped with a church camp, and a well-studied Bible professor was leading a class called "The Ideal Christian." On the very first day, he wisely informed his students that the best way to become an ideal Christian is to study the life of Christ himself. For the next week, we took several chapters of Matthew each day and wrote down everything we saw Jesus doing. You could imagine the list was long by the end of the week. Although this exercise was so simple, it was so profound. I would challenge you to try it. Read one chapter a day in Matthew and write down on a notecard the things you see Jesus doing in the text, then do your best that day to emulate Christ. I bet you will quickly start to see that it is a tall order indeed, but worth the effort.

To Be Like Christ Is To Be A Servant:

Many attributes can be ascribed to Christ, but I think to be like Christ is to be a servant-leader. In our world today, everyone wants to lead, but few want to serve. As a culture, we have readily embraced self-government and self-morality. Relativism trains us to believe that we are in charge of determining morality and has led us to a path of refuting authority. We don't want anyone telling us what to do, and the God-ordained attribute of knowing how to submit to someone else got thrown to the wolves. We each want to dictate our own destiny and somehow forget that we do not live in isolation so we cannot feasibly all endorse self-autonomy. So, we look around us and see countless examples of self-service and carving our own personal paths to the life we deem successful without seeing how very selfish we have all become.

Christ was selfless. He lived to serve others to the extent of giving His very life just so you and I could keep ours. Lauren Daigle says it this way, "You plead my cause. You right my wrongs. You break my chains. You overcome. You gave your life to give me mine. You say that I am free. How can it be?"

How can that be? Because he loves, He loves to serve others first.

Angie radiates the love of Christ to the people of our church and her community. Her most obvious spiritual gift is encouragement. I cannot begin to count how many cards Mrs. Angie sends every week, year after year after year, to anyone who may need some sense of joy. She spends her life serving others.

Joe radiates God's love to the people at his work. He seems to always have a story about someone at his work and how God provided an opportunity to just have honest conversations about their doubts towards faith. Joe could see his factory job as something to endure, but instead He sees it every day as a privilege to find ways to share God with a broken world.

Irma radiates service quietly, faithfully, behind the scenes every single week in our church. She willingly undertakes mundane tasks and completes them week after week, month after month, year after year. She plays weekly with the worship team with very little notice, and yet she eagerly anticipates one more week where she gets to serve.

Jose radiates servant-leadership every moment of his life as he uses his God-given talents to lead others to Christ. He rarely sleeps because the harvest is plentiful, but the workers are few. And when you meet him, you immediately sense a deep love for Christ and an earnest passion to reach the lost. From miracles to the mundane, Jose pours his life out as an offering to our Great God.

What about you? Are you radiating God's love through your service?

If you want to be like Christ, get your hands dirty. If you want to be like Christ, do something quietly for someone else with the hope of no one noticing. If you want to be like Christ, quit living for yourself.

To Be Like Christ Is To Choose Holiness Over Happiness:

The American culture I experience is saturated with entertainment. It seems that most people clock into a job so they can make money to eventually spend on vacations or toys. Be honest for a moment with yourself and evaluate your own life. If you had to record the ways you spend your time and the ways you spend your money, are you depositing more into your own account or God's?

Some time back, I wrote the following for our church newsletter, and it seems fitting to share:

Happiness or Holiness

We live in a morally relative culture that tries to convince us our lives are our own and our purpose is to find the things in this world that make us happy and pursue them.

We put up with our jobs so we can then get out of that daily imprisonment and go do the things we enjoy like scrolling our social media, taking our kids to their events, watching our shows on Netflix, dining out with our people, going on our family vacations, enjoying our days off...all in attempts to make us happy. But did you notice the key word in all of those? It was the first-person pronoun our.

What if we lived out our lives using only third person pronouns, focusing on others and not ourselves?

Let's do a quick self-check:

- *Do you see your job as an obligation or a ministry?*
- *When was the last time you reached out to the sick, the widows, the orphans, the imprisoned, the broken?*
- *What do you look forward to more: a day of doing whatever you want or a day of encouraging others?*
- *When was the last time you shared life with a nonbeliever?*

1 Peter 1:14-15 (ESV) says, "As obedient children, do not be conformed to the passions of your former ignorance, but as he who called you is holy, you also be holy in all your conduct."

Jesus set the standard for holy conduct by sacrificially and unconditionally loving others, so what if we quit making excuses and simply did as Jesus did, loving others every possible chance we got? What would our lives look like if we traded in our personal passions for compassion?

In other words, what if God-centered holiness mattered more than self-centered happiness?

If you want to be like Christ, choose holiness over happiness. Be like Him who tells his disciples, who tells us, "Whoever wants to become great among you must be your servant, and whoever wants to be first must be slave of all. For even the Son of Man did not come to be served, but to serve, and to give his life as a ransom for many" (Mark 10:43-45, NIV).

Know in advance that living a life of servant-leadership will be harder than you can imagine, but you won't ever have to do it alone. Know in advance that the joy of serving alongside Him will far outweigh any hardship you encounter along the way, along "The Way."

To Be Like Christ Is To Submit:

I was teaching an Honors class at MCHS, and a select group of students were in the front of the class conducting a debate on feminism. When I assign a class debate, I try to mediate only, but if one group is struggling to the point of embarrassment, I have been known to come to the rescue to keep the debate going.

In this instance, one group was throwing out fiery darts to their opponents to no avail, and I was watching for an opportunity to intervene. When they suddenly brought up submission as a weakness for their next argument, I saw my chance.

Rather calmly, I asked to interject one small question. I then asked, "Have you ever submitted to something and found it easy, because the last time I checked, submission requires immense strength?"

Silence.

They knew it was true. Our culture tries to convince us that submission is weak, but any fool can stop and see that submitting my will to the will of someone else requires intense power. As a daughter, wife, mom, friend, I often find myself wanting things my way all while knowing I need to let God direct and think of others before myself. That, my friend, is at the heart of submission: thinking of others more than you think of yourself.

Living a life of submission to God is one of the hardest things I do on the daily. It is also one of the best things I do. For over a year now, a prominent mantra in my life has been open hands and open heart. I have been asking God to put the things into my life that He wants me to hold and to take the things out He no longer asks me to carry.

Amid a pandemic, this has been more difficult than I predicted. Then we took in a friend who needed a place to stay. My oldest two children are down to months before they head off to college and life. My mom is nearing death after twenty-seven years of one health issue after another. I have so many things I want to hold onto, but over and over again, God reminds me that submission is best.

Submission is best. It always has been and it always will be. Jesus himself submitted to God by going to the cross just for you and just for me. If we really want to be a Christian, someone who lives like Him, then we must be willing to go to any extreme God asks of us. It will be the way to true life.

Reflection Questions:

1. Are you a Christian?
2. If you are a Christian, how would someone who encounters you know without you telling them?
3. If you aren't a Christian, what is holding you back?

Meet Me Here

~sHe~

She was too young with a veiled clarity for the blackened white amid swirling greys, but we probably shouldn't blame her-a habit of youth. She blames herself enough already.

You came. Soft, slow, seducing. So she gave. Every last ounce of her heart and soul, and then the final prized token of her unfailing devotion so you would finally know her love. Her first and final Hail Mary.

She never was the same.

Times broken pieces to put humpty dumpty back together again, and just when she thought all was healed, you dropped in again.

Why here at her own home church of all places? The teeter-totter of mind over emotion, knowing this is the exact place she wants you to be, but your arrival seemingly caused the ground to fall away beneath her, and she doesn't quite know how to get back up. The Jekyll of wanting you to know Christ like you have never known him before but the Hyde of wishing you would have chosen somewhere else to take your pursuing heart.

Why would God do such a thing?

Yes, I know. You have great plans for me. Really, You do. And it is insane how You are doing a good thing in me through all the debased pits of my weeping heart. So, I do hear You. Really, I do.

You know how I have struggled with this for some time now. You know how I want so much for this to not be a big deal, but then within seconds it is erupting inside bigger than life, and then I just don't know how to breathe. Spirit and flesh battling inside for the final victory over how I will go on with life now that his presence is in my midst.

Life does go on, and we live in the here and now. I cannot recreate the past with all its veiled clarity, but I can use the vivid picture You have revealed today to move past this moment. I am not defined by my past. I must trust that You alone can show Him truth and think not of the me he knew but choose instead to see the me You have made me to be. But really, it is not me at all he needs to see; it is You we all need.

I will choose in this moment to step out of my pit of pity, for pity really is the base for my wallowed pit. And I will live in the spirit over the flesh, knowing You clothe me with righteousness and see not all the wretched shame of my past. When I stand in Your fathomless glory, I fall to pieces inside because I am reminded of how very unworthy I am. His presence reminds me of my guilt-choosing his Hail Mary over the bloodied sacrifice of my Jesus. But I no longer live that life of lies, and though it haunts me still daily, I am not defined by the veiled past. Satan would try to tell me differently, but as we sang today, when the lies speak louder than the truth, remind me I belong to you.

I cried a lot today. Weeping for the past that I cannot alter and for how much You love me despite me. And if I am honest, weeping also for all the he's whose hearts I played around with in my down-spiraling implosion of youth. I was a blackened mess. But You pulled me from the muck and mire and gave me a new name, so I can either sink into the regret of the past or embrace the hope of a future You offer freely, a gift I can never earn but desperately need.

I will take your offering. I will kneel at the altar of Your love because it is the only place I can be whole again, and I will gladly welcome him to do the same even if it is in my midst, because that is Your desire, and all I want is to have Your heart.

EIGHT

SPEAK TO ME

Anticipation Questions:

1. How would you describe prayer?
2. When should we pray?
3. How should we pray?

Psalm 5:1-3 (NIV)-" Give ear to my words, O Lord, consider my sighing. Listen to my cry for help, my King and my God, for to you I pray. In the morning, O Lord, you hear my voice; in the morning I lay my requests before you and wait in expectation."

Philippians 4:6-7 (NIV)-" Do not be anxious about anything, but in everything, by prayer and petition, with thanksgiving, present your requests to God. And the peace of God, which transcends all understanding, will guard your hearts and your minds in Christ Jesus."

Dear Abba Father,

I am sitting here in my chair in quiet solitude, just me and you. When I sat to pray before writing this chapter, I sensed you saying what better way to talk about prayer than to just talk to me about it. So here I am.

If I am being honest, I could feel a little unsure about this whole endeavor because you know that sometimes my prayers are full of heart cries to you, and this one feels a little bit like I should stay focused, write with concision and clarity, and make sure what you want them to know is apparent.

But then again, You can do much more in talking truth into them than I ever could, so why am I even worried.

God, my prayer life has been rocky at best. I guess I didn't realize how inconsistent it was until I started watching Katherine in her own prayer life.

Just the other day we were talking about her great transformation. The middle school Katherine who sighed every time we breathed it seemed became the brilliant, vibrant in her faith Katherine to the point where anyone who encounters her cannot help but notice her genuine outpouring of You to everyone she encounters.

God, I have such a long way to go.

I am not naturally kind to others. I get defensive easily. I am frustrated with others when they don't behave the way I think they should. I am impatient at times and oh, God, I am far from who I want to be. But Katherine, Katherine lives it well already.

When Katherine and I were talking about what helped her change, she immediately pointed to you. Her huge Holy Spirit moment in 2019 at CIY moved mountains for her. God, I could arise every day for the rest of my life to thank you for doing that in her and still never express how grateful I am for the way You changed her life.

I know You have changed my life as well, even as I don't always see it. I can look back on the high school Lesa and wonder why anyone liked me at all.... And then as I fly over the years since then, I see countless ways I have simply failed to show Your love.

God, I don't want to be a failure. And it's not for the same reasons it used to be. I used to hate failure because I didn't want to look "less." But that was all about me. Now I don't want to be a failure because I don't want to miss opportunities to be Your hands and feet to the very hurting world around me.

God, when I look around me, I see so many hurting people. I see people who deny you, people who claim you in name only, and people who love you fully. I want to be in love with You and You alone.

When I was a younger girl, I heard someone talk about Mother Teresa. As they told stories of the way she lived her life, I was inspired by her great selflessness. I have no recollection of where I was or who was speaking, but I remember they said that Mother Teresa told people that life should be a constant prayer. And it struck me hard.

What does that even mean? At that time, I thought it was an absurd thought because my idea of prayer was very limited. I thought prayer meant the times I closed my eyes and bowed my head and asked You to bless my food. Or it was the times when I closed my eyes and bowed my head during Sunday School or a church service so we could ask You to help people who were sick.

But I know more and more that prayer is much bigger than all of that. God, I see prayer as an open path between me and you where everything I do, everything I think, everything I say is a direct outpouring of You flowing in me and through me.

Prayer was never meant to be an occasion; prayer is supposed to be a posture. A relationship with You does not mean that I sometimes consult You when I am desperate or have a to-do list for You. Prayer is not where I finally decide to give You the time of day and put You on a stopwatch because I have other things on my agenda for the day.

Prayer in its basic form is communication. When I google its definition, I get lots of answers, but one I appreciate is "an invocation or act that seeks to activate a rapport with an object of worship through deliberate communication." If I am deliberate about my relationship with You, then I will constantly seek to build a rapport with You by talking to You all the time.

Whoever thinks prayer is only when we bow our heads and close our eyes is a fool.

God, I don't want to limit my relationship with You to a few times a day. I need You to go with me EVERYWHERE. I need You to lead me through it all. Lead me through the green pastures; lead me by the still waters; lead me through the valley of the shadow of death; lead me through to the mountain summit. God, everywhere, all the time, stay with me.

God, I have felt so lonely in my life. Even now I can get into a funk and feel rather out of touch with others even as they are in the very room where I am moving through life. But the truth is that You are always with me, and Your rod and staff promise to always comfort me no matter what I may be going through. And God, sometimes life is just so very hard. Sometimes I have no idea where I am going or what I am supposed to do.

But you know.

God, You know me inside and out. You knitted me together in my mama's womb and you have counted the hairs on my head. You know every single thing about me and yet You love me still. Why wouldn't I want to invite Your presence into every single second I live on this earth…

It's what I want, and yet I fail. Too often I go about my day with moments of forgetfulness. For sure I am obsessed with thoughts about You more today than in years past, and for that I am so grateful. In some ways, it reminds me of when Daniel and I were first dating. I was consumed by thoughts of him. I think we all relate to that in some way. When we fall in love, we cannot help but think about the significant other. God, help us fall in love with You even deeper still.

Consume me. Make me obsessed with You. Move in me so that my entire life is a constant prayer, a constant cry to You to be part of every single thing I do. God, make my prayer life come alive with the author of life itself.

God, I want my whole life to radiate Yours. I want to die so much to myself that Your Spirit becomes bright in me like a blazing wildfire. God, I want others to see You when they see me. Help me to get over myself each and every day so that I may get on to You and Your glory.

And God, I pray this also for every single person who will read this. If that is just one person, I pray it for him or her earnestly. God, let us stop giving lip service to You. It is my heart's cry for everyone who needs You, and God, I know we all need you. Desperately, fervently, ardently…

"I need you, oh I need you. Every hour I need you, my one defense, my righteousness, Oh God how I need You."[10]

So please teach my song to rise to You. Teach me something new every day so I will grow more and more in love with You. When others attack, or when I self-attack mentally with dark thoughts, be my defense to speak Truth into me. Make me right in You by knowing You more.

God, my prayer is weak at best. I do not rise every day to greet You. The lulls of my phone distract me from finding You first. So here I am asking you to work it out in me. Help me to lay my life before you every morning and wait expectantly for You to respond.

God, help my life be a constant prayer with You as the center of everything I do.

In Jesus's holy and precious name, Amen.

Dear friend, I don't know where you are in your talks with God. You may have decided you can't even stand the sound of His name... Or maybe you just don't really know Him and have no idea where to start. Maybe it feels odd to talk to someone who is not tangibly in Your presence, or maybe you are like I was and grew up believing prayer is confined to certain times and events. Regardless of where you are, I know where God is and that is everywhere at all times. He is in the air you breathe; He is all around you. He sees your every move, and He is just waiting to have a deeper relationship with You.

Friend, please open the door for communication. Don't be afraid to be honest with Him, and don't hesitate to talk out your doubts and fears and insecurities with Him. He is the safest place you can go, and He is the only one who will never leave you nor forsake you. And His love, oh the rich depths of His love will become more and more real to you the more you talk with Him and invite Him into every corner of your life.

---

[10] Maher, Matt. "Lord, I Need You." *All the People Said Amen,* Provident Label Group LLC, 2013. Spotify, open.spotify.com/track/4EHWldZTas5KUyFtT0rQlY.

Do you have things in the dark corners of your life you hesitate to show others? He already knows it's there. He wants to walk with you to those areas and shine His light onto it so you can see it is not nearly as scary as you thought. Monsters under the bed are only frightening to His children when we are sitting in the dark. But when you cry out to Him to come to your side, He will turn on the light and dispel the darkness. You really have nothing to fear if God is with you.

So pray. Pray right now. Pray when you are brushing your teeth. Pray when you are eating. Pray even as you are sharing life with others. Invite God into every part of your life and watch every part of your life be transformed. It will be nothing less than beautiful, I promise.

Reflection Quest:

1. Take twenty minutes. Put your phone on silence and away from you. Write out a prayer or pray out loud, spending this time talking to God. Remember that a conversation means moments of talking AND moments of listening. Still your heart. Still your mind. Spend time in His presence.

Meet Me Here

-A Recovering Atheist-

My mom has a picture of me in the nursery at our church, and I am sitting with several other babies who would be my primary friends for the first sixteen years of my life. You see, I grew up in church. I cannot recall a time not knowing church and church things. Most of my memories entail some element of a church event. But as Craig Groeschel would say, I am a recovering Christian atheist.[11] I read my bible some, prayed some, went to church often.

High school hit and things got a little more complicated, largely because I had been obsessed with boys since fourth grade. By the time I was a junior, we moved to a new town, and within a year, my mom had an accident at work. By the time senior year was finishing up, I was desperate for something stable in my life, and that stability came in the form of my boyfriend. After an intense heartbreak, I found myself floundering in my faith; I was a "hot mess."

A semester in Oxford helped me find God again; a bible study with our youth pastor's wife helped me learn how to study my bible; a young mom who moved into town and became my dear friend taught me how to pray; a mentor showed me how to have hard conversations to save my marriage; a ranch in Montana showed me how to serve with my whole heart.

I am so very blessed. God has divinely orchestrated people and places just so I could see Him more clearly. How could I ever go back now, and how could I not share the vision with others?

---

[11] Groeschel, Craig. *The Christian Atheist: Believing in God but Living as If He Doesn't Exist.* Zondervan, 2010.

NINE

THE CHURCH LIES

Anticipation Questions:

1. What should the church look like?
2. What is one stronghold you struggle with?
3. Why should you go to church?

The cultural climate seems to be rapidly moving away from Christian values in our present day, and I cannot help but notice numerous Christians scratching their heads, wondering how we suddenly got here. As a history teacher who can see the beginnings of this transition in the 50s and 60s, I am not quite as baffled. Honestly, the church has been asleep in a lot of ways for a very long time, and we are the ones encountering a "woke" moment more than the culture itself. Perhaps without intention, the church has propagated untruths for quite some time that landed it in a culture aggressively attacking it more and more each day, and the church is far from innocent. We have been "lying" far too long.

Lie #1: Faith is About Me

I was a young adult when the worship wars reigned hot and heavy in most American churches. For years, traditional hymns rang loud and clear in sanctuaries until the worship music industry began to evolve after artists like Michael W. Smith and Amy Grant made big waves. As the years progressed and the music industry continued to morph into a much larger entity, countless opportunities arose for "modern" worship music to make its way into the walls of church buildings.

Some liked it; some did not. Thus were birthed the worship wars, where congregations would split over the style of music played during service. And just a side note as food for thought, the very term church service denotes serving others; very little service arose from churches entangled in the web of music preference.

My point here is not to debate worship styles, but rather to illustrate a larger point; for too many people in too many churches, the focus has been on self and not on God. At the root of worship wars or any war over the style of service is an integral insistence on self. Yet God calls us to love Him, love others, and serve both. We even say I am going to attend a church service, and yet walk through the doors expecting to be served.

In John F. Kennedy's inaugural address, he states, "Ask not what your country can do for you-ask what you can do for your country." These infamous words became a national mantra passed down for generations to come, and the same principle should apply for God's people. We should not ask what a church service can do for us; we should ask how we can use a church service to serve others.

For years I have doubted the effectiveness of our current church service. If God intends us to serve Him and others, and we even call our Sunday gatherings a service, then why does very little time get spent doing just that? Instead, we Christians have adopted a democratic, consumer mentality when it comes to church. First, we have the right to vote on everything because we can't trust God to work all things for good for those who love Him. Second, we have the right to consume an event every Sunday morning that makes us feel like we have done our part for the week so we can go about our daily, worldly lives for the next six days.

The I is a bit overbearing here, and the me in it all naturally secludes God from the picture. We are either for Him or against Him, and being against Him is subtly easier for us to swallow than we likely care to admit.

Faith is not about me. It never has been, and it never will be. God in His goodness invites me to be part of His story, but it is HIS STORY. And when I act out because I don't get my way, it is no wonder that those seekers sitting next to me suddenly quit attending.

Jesus spoke the most harshly to a set of people in his time-the Pharisees and the Sadducees. These men were considered the most holy in their time, and yet Jesus was ruthless to them, even calling them children of Satan. Why were they children of Satan? You and I are either a child of God or a child of Satan, so if we are not living a life for Christ, we are living a life for ourselves. Living for self means we are in Satan's camp because that is exactly how he lives as well-it's all about me.

Maybe it is time we quit thinking so much about ourselves. Maybe it is time we think about others and how we can give them the greatest gift in all of history, the truth of God. Maybe it is also time we quit arranging church events around our personal desires and make it what we call it, a time of service.

Lie # 2: Get it Together

Matthew West wrote a song entitled "Truth be Told," and in that song, he says that the church has proposed lie # 1 that says we are "supposed to have it all together. And when they ask how you're doin', just smile and tell them, 'Never better.'" He goes on to talk about lie number two, which claims that "Everybody's life is perfect except yours so keep your messes and your wounds and your secrets safe with you behind closed doors." Both coincide into one major lie the church sometimes propagates: Christians have it all together.

I do not have it all together. Neither do you. When left to myself, I am a mess, and so are you. But when I invite God to move in and inhabit me fully, I take on a new identity. I become His. And when the God of the universe lives in me, then suddenly I am a much different creature, redeemed…but still messy.

The problem with the message the church sends out, even if unintentionally, is that you don't really belong in church with those put-together Christians if you are not put together. So, you need to get it together in order to hang with them. But that is not at all what we see of Jesus when He lived here on earth. He very much preferred to hang with the sinners, the sideliners, the overlooked and underprivileged. Yet so much of our modern America church has seemed more comfortable for those who could put on their Sunday best with their roast at home in the crockpot. Not everyone can afford some Sunday best, much less a crockpot with a roast. And so, they felt out of place in our buildings. And what do we do to make sure we are presenting Jesus's message of love and acceptance? We walk into our buildings, claiming we are attending a service that just serves self, and then we walk out of those buildings into the comforts of our home behind closed doors once again.

Closed doors close off God. It is time we open it all up so God can move as He wills through us. Admitting we don't have it all together may just save our lives, and others along the way.

Does anyone have it all together? Absolutely not, but I know the One who holds all things together, and I so want you to know Him too. My friend, He is worth living for, and worth dying for. So, every day I do my best to die to self and life for Christ. Paul was spot on when he said, "To live is Christ, and to die is gain" (Philippians 1:21, NIV). I hope the same for you and for me, even as we don't have it all together.

Lie # 3: Church Participation ≠ Christian Sanctification

In Sunday School this morning, we were working through a chapter about what the Bible says about loving God from Summit's *Understanding the Faith* textbook. The lesson talked about the Frank Sinatra song that was penned by Henry Wadsworth Longfellow during the Civil War, shortly after he lost his second wife (his first wife and daughter were his former tragic losses). Longfellow contemplates how there can be peace on earth, and he comes to this conclusion: God is not dead nor doth he sleep.

In *The Chronicles of Narnia*, Aslan represents God for C. S. Lewis in the form of a lion. The beaver reminds us that this lion, this Aslan, is not safe but He is good. All throughout these chronicled adventures, we see Aslan weaving in and out of the narrative, but never once do the main characters who know Him mistake him for a passive lion. Oh no, Aslan, even in his seeming absence, is far from inactive, truly representing the God I serve. My God is not dead, nor does He sleep.

This Aslan God was not the character I learned about as I grew up. I knew God was big; I knew God was in control; I knew God was the creator of all things. I did not know God is alive and in the business of transforming us, bringing dead things back to life. You know why I didn't know this? It is because I sat Sunday after Sunday surrounded by people who were the walking dead. Their church participation led to a lot of information, but what I needed, what we all need, is transformation which leads to sanctification.

When I was a little girl, my mom started taking us to church even though my dad did not attend. Sometime into this arrangement, my dad started to come, so that by the time I was old enough to remember, we were a good, church-going family. We rarely missed a Sunday, we served at pretty much every function the church offered, and we faithfully attended our local church camp every summer. God was certainly hanging around our lives, but I am not convinced He was invited to be the central part of everything we said and did. And although I am beyond grateful that my parents raised me in church, I am also saddened that we all missed out, my parents included…and if I am honest my own kids in my own home as well for a long time.

See, I grew up believing this was what it meant to be a Christian. As long as I attended church functions consistently, behaved like a good, moral citizen in my community, and gave my 10% to God's work, then I was living a Godly life.

I was living a lie.

As I sat down this evening to write this chapter, I asked God to lead me to something He wanted to share. I flipped to 2 Chronicles and started reading. As I began chapter twenty-five, I learned about a man named Amaziah. Amaziah was twenty-five when he became king and verse two tells us that, "He did what was right in the eyes of the Lord, but not wholeheartedly" (NIV). The chapter goes on to relate how he did some good things, but because his heart was not in the right spot, he ended up a prideful man who met his death because he had turned away from following God. Where did he go wrong? He had a divided heart.

The church I grew up in and the church I serve in now can harbor people who have a divided heart. If I can be transparent, they are some of my favorite people who have done immeasurably good things for me and my family. I think this is likely why I never doubted their living testimony to what it means to be a Christian. Because they are such good people, I assumed they had this whole faith thing figured out. What I couldn't figure out was why for years I still felt so very lost.

For years I felt something was missing, especially when I turned to scripture and read stories about people like Paul or Job or James or Moses. These men were the real deal. Far from perfect, they still lived a life on full mission for God once He got a hold of them. I just kept waiting for my own time to come, and for God to get a hold of me.

God did not get a hold of me in the church pew, and sadly enough, I am not sure the church pews in my current church always offer the most promise for finding Him either. It is hard to find God's very living water flowing out of church attenders whose lives indicate lethargic apathy for God's global mission.

Just today a new friend of mine was talking about how she was never really interested in politics before, but now she finds herself immersed in them. She related that she believes that may be the heart of the issue; for too long we sat uninvolved in too many arenas because it didn't impact us close to home. Now that the secular world is bearing down on our doorsteps, we Christians have decided to take a stand and cannot begin to fathom how we ever got here. We likely got here because we naively believed our faith was deep while we happily slept in the comforts of our shallow shalom.

Casting Crowns shares these lyrics in their song "While You Were Sleeping:"

> United States of America
> Looks like another silent night
> As we're sung to sleep by philosophies
> That save the trees and kill the children
> America, what will we miss while we are sleeping

The church of America has been too silent for too long, but why? Is it possible that the church has been lying down on the job because of a theological lie at the root of its foundation? Have we bought the bait that we really can halfway do life with Christ?

I struggle with our daily heresies. I struggle with the daily heresy of church goers. I also struggle with the years of lost opportunity because of my own heresy. One reason why I struggle with heretical lives is because of the people I am trying to reach. I cannot count how many people I have recently tried to share life with, in hopes of them considering a road toward Jesus, only to find them completely turned off by any mention of religion because of heretical people-the ones who act righteous without actually being submissive in any way to God's work in their life. Do I still fall short? Absolutely, but that is not heresy. According to the Cambridge dictionary, heresy is "an action that shows you have no respect for the official opinion." In this case, the "official opinion" is God's which makes it a fact. And the fact is, people are always responsible for their own salvation, but we too are commanded in the scriptures to impact the people in our world. And if we believe that church attendance alone is enough to impact others, then we are living a lie.

The church lies sleeping and has done so for years because we have bought the lie that we can have our cake and eat it too. Revelation 3:14-18 (NIV) says:

> "To the angel of the church in Laodicea write: These are the words of the Amen, the faithful and true witness, the ruler of God's creation. I know your

> deeds, that you are neither cold nor not. I wish you were either one or the other! So, because you are lukewarm-neither hot nor cold, I am about to spit you out of my mouth. You say, 'I am rich; I have acquired wealth and do not need a thing.' But you do not realize that you are wretched, pitiful, poor, blind, and naked. I counsel you to buy from me gold refined in the fire, so you can become rich; and white clothes to wear, so you can cover your shameful nakedness; and salve to put on your eyes so you can see."

God makes it clear that we cannot ride the fence and expect His goodness, yet I see so very many around me doing this very thing, and honestly, I too am guilty as charged.

Please hear that very loud and clear-I too am guilty as charged. I recognize that this chapter especially can seem very critical of people I dearly love. My intent is not to criticize or condemn; I do hope, however, that we are all convicted. Even as I write these harsh words, my heart aches for the church family of my youth and members in my current church family (Note: in all church families that I have been blessed by, I can name numerous individuals who absolutely were living out God's truth, so please know this is not at all a comprehensive inclusion). As God has revealed new ideas of what it really means to be the church, I have fallen to my knees in shame for the ways I have behaved without even recognizing fault, and I fully believe the same goes for the very people in my church whom I love dearly. I am not sure they have ever seen church life any other way than the mediocrity the are living, and all the while they believe they are offering a life of chocolates when they are at best offering broccoli.

God offers so much more than mediocrity. For years, I prayed and prayed that my Christian faith would grow, but I did nothing more than keep up my good attendance record and serve diligently all while spending more time in my week thinking about myself than about God. If we really want to be transformed into who God wants us to be, then maybe we should spend more time around him since what we worship greatly impacts what we become. If I worship my own time or my worldly pleasures, I will remain worldly. If I worship the holy, living, transcendent and immanent God, I will become more Godly.

When Jesus leaves this earth, his last words are a great commission for us to go into all nations. When the Holy Spirit descends upon Jesus's people on the day of Pentecost, we see that the people there were not all locals. Acts 2:5-6 (NIV) says, "Now there were staying in Jerusalem God-fearing Jews from every nation under heaven. When they heard this sound, a crowd came together in bewilderment, because each one heard them speaking in his own language." Did you see it? From the birth of the church, God set His people on a global mission, actively pursuing a Godly life that points others to do the same. There is nothing mediocre about this call.

If you are already professing Christ, are you on mission, all in? Are you living a life that dwells more in the me sphere or the Spirit sphere? Are you like Mother Teresa who said her entire life was a constant prayer because everything she did was in communication with God? Did you know every moment of every day really can be God-centered? Even when you eat or go to the bathroom or study for an exam or take out the trash or clock into work, you can invite God into that part of your story so that EVERYTHING you do, you do it for the glory of God.

It is time to show the world that the American church has been asleep too long, living the lie that we can be part-time Christians.

I used to be a part-time Christian. What this really meant was I was someone who was a good, moral citizen and claimed Christ, but I was not even part-time His if I am being honest. Scripture reminds us we cannot be part anything when it comes to faith. We really are either in or out. If I have really encountered His grace and mercy and love, I cannot help but want to live more for Him and be all in. And the more I encounter Him, the more I want Him, and the more I want Him, the more I seek and find Him. This in turn means I am encountering Him more and more and more and I hope you see the pattern. All it takes is one step toward Him, recognizing that you quite possibly have believed a lie all these years thinking that church participation equates personal sanctification.

When I look back on all the years I bought the lie, I am very saddened because I can see how much I was missing. I am far from perfect today, and I will be the first to tell you that I have a lot to learn about who my God is, but I can also see abundant growth towards Him. I desperately want the same for my fellow church attendees. I want us all to bask in the abundant life God offers to us when we go all in with Him. If you aren't all in, you are missing out on so much, and I just really want you to experience what I have experienced, a life full of Him, even as I fall short.

Go all in. Today. Wholeheartedly. Make the jump, splash into the unknown, and one day you will be able to look back to see how you walked on water with Him. Please don't miss the life He is offering. Don't settle for church participation when God offers real sanctification- the act of making something holy...the act of God making You, my friend, Holy and His.

Reflection Questions:

1. If you could recreate church services, what would they look like?
2. What is an additional lie the church propagates, either knowingly or unknowingly?
3. How has the church hurt you?

Meet Me Here

~Victims of Love~

I once had a student who wrote about her molester. Raw, tender, beautiful young girl whose deacon touched her in bad places. Told her not to tell. My throat screams injustice as my stomach churns with the thought of the injustice she has endured.

She was a victim of child molestation. But is she really a victim?

Racism breeds its hot hatred year after year, day after day. Moment after moment we are bombarded with the clashing tension. Blacks demanding a voice in a world that has historically oppressed, and whites screaming back that we live only in the present and cannot be held accountable for the sins of our fathers. Spouting ignorance about the realities of cultural degradation runs rampant in all of us. We are all victims of our upbringings, buying into the abcs of our youth. But are we really victims?

My husband and I talked about this the other night. Black, white, rich, poor-so few change from what they have known. Stuck in the cycles of the familiar, we may venture a bit from the nucleus but fail to find implosion that launches us into brand-new spheres of orbits.

I guess I see it like this. It is easy for me to sit in my comfortable life and throw stones at someone else and tell them their poverty or their depravity is their own fault, believing that if they would only work harder, they would rise above their situation. The honest reality is even the richest white man rarely moves beyond his own situation in which he was raised to fill. We often live impressed under the cultural norms of whatever life has looked like day in day out. We fail to move beyond what we know because we are victims who lack courage and strength and perseverance to make a change. But does it have to be like this? Are we really victims?

As a Christian, my default is to take all questions to the context of how God would answer this question. And as often happens, he points me to the cross.

Jesus was the ultimate victim. Bruised and beaten for his perfection, outcast for belonging to God, rejected for refusing to follow the norm, he died for me to pay my price and set an example for me to fall hard into. From every angle I look, Jesus was a victim. But He would deny every ounce of that claim. He says we are only victims if we choose the flesh. When we choose the spirit, we are never a victim. Through His Spirit, we step outside the flesh into a life where nothing that happens to our flesh can destroy what He has done in our Spirit, and it is then that all people-black, white, rich, poor-move beyond victimization and into abundant life.

Blacks and white alike, if they choose secular over spirit, are all victims who frustrate the progression of life. Choosing the part of the victim leaves us unable to make a change, so we displace responsibility and live stagnantly blaming others with no hope of rising above our circumstances.

My student is no different. Her flesh was victimized-cruel, heartless beast of a man who took advantage of her. Every part of me cries sorrow for what has happened to her, but I would do her an injustice if I simply offered a tissue with no hope for something better. But, I do have something better-hope for a life outside this flesh that draws us closer to eternal life with every passing breath. I can offer her life in the spirit that rises above all the miseries of this world.

It is only when we embrace the love Jesus offered us on that cross that we can be anything more than the filth of the life around us. This same sweet promise applies to us all-from the privileged white man residing in a white house to the colored man kneeling on the grass. We are all victims of the flesh who desperately need to choose to live life in the spirit and be a different kind of victim-a victim of love.

TEN

THE CULTURE LIES

Anticipation Questions:

1. Why would someone avoid Christianity?
2. Does absolute morality exist? How do you know?
3. How do science and faith go together?

Who is the authority of your life?

If you are reading this as a believer, your immediate answer was hopefully God. If you are a nonbeliever reading this book, you likely answered "me." A believer must question if he really lives every moment of every day as if God really holds authority over his whole life. The nonbeliever, if he is honest, should be able to detect various influences on his life that dictate his choices. Regardless of our theological philosophies, the reality of authority in our daily lives eludes a definitive outcome.

Living in a postmodern world brings a plethora of ideology, and moral relativism rests at the top of this philosophical era. What exactly is moral relativism? We have talked about it several times already, but for a recap, one way to define it is to say what is good for me is good for me, and what is good for you is good for you, or in other words, you do you and I'll do me. A more technical definition is that no absolute moral truth exists for everyone in all places at all times. Truth with a capital "T" simply ceases to exist in the postmodern world.

Although many living in the twenty-first century might believe the denial of Truth and the push for moral relativism is a recent phenomenon, they are wrong. The Stanford Encyclopedia of Philosophy states, "Though moral relativism did not become a prominent topic in philosophy or elsewhere until the twentieth century, it has ancient origins. In the classical Greek world, both the historian Herodotus and the sophist Protagoras appeared to endorse some form of relativism (the latter attracted the attention of Plato in the *Theaetetus*)." Moral relativism finds its root in ancient philosophy even as it rears his head towards dominance in the modern era.

Why has moral relativism gained such prominence in recent times? Many reasons exist, but for our purposes, let's consider one aspect of this puzzle. Should it surprise us that a society that began to insist that God is dead would land in the camp of moral relativism? When culture decides God does not exist, authority automatically flies out the door. Since God is the authority and all other authority derives its power from Him, a claim against His existence would naturally eliminate all other authority. When authority ceases to exist, the only entity left for decision-making is me, myself, and I. By its very definition, authority implies power of one person or group over another. So, without authority, all that is left is the individual other, which then leads naturally to this person determining all truths for herself, hence you do you and I'll do me.

What do we do when we believe no ultimate authority exists? We create our own rules of engagement that are self-serving. It seems that every argument the culture propagates against faith stems from this self-pleasing, morally-relative realm.

Argument Against Christianity- Claim Number 1:
Christianity arrogantly claims to be the only truth.

My friend Jaxon, whom I mentioned earlier, believes Christianity claims to be the only way when so many other ideas are equally merited.

Christianity certainly feels exclusive. It doesn't help when people who claim Christ in name also act like they are better than everyone else simply because they got wet and know some Bible stories. Who wants to be part of a group who claim to have the love of God in them all while living lives that look much like the rest of their community? I know it turns me off, and I fully believe God is real and try to live a daily life of surrender to His will.

Let's look more closely at Jaxon's theology. He claims he would never want to devote himself fully to a worldview, and yet even in saying that he is fully devoted to this worldview he has created. We are all fully devoted to whatever worldview we are believing in for the moment, even if the basic tenets are shifting daily. You can't not have a worldview. And if each one of us has a worldview, then we each are fully devoting ourselves to living out behaviors based on that worldview. So, if I believe that all religions are equally good in what they stand for, then that is my own "religion," and every action I choose for my life flows from that ideological belief, including the fact that he is claiming his worldview to be right and my worldview to be wrong. His statement implies that he struggles with a religion/worldview that would claim another to be wrong, but even this very statement implies that he is right, and I am wrong, which means he is condemning himself in practice. If he has a hard time looking at people who would claim others are wrong, then he has a hard time looking at himself because the very statement that this worldview of "tolerance" is the right one implies that any other is wrong. In the name of tolerance, he too is intolerant. What he really wants is to be able to say that what he personally believes is true and what you personally believe is true; you do you and I'll do me, and we'll pretend to agree under the pretense of tolerance even as we don't actually agree with one another.

The main difference between a moral relativist then and a Christian is the claim for truth. Moral relativists are no different than Christians as far as having a worldview that does not align with the neighbor next door, but because as they say I am fine with you having your worldview and me having mine, they believe they are different from Christians even as they aren't. They still have worldviews that don't align. The difference lies on the surface only in the realm of rhetoric. Take two non-Christians whose worldviews don't align. They claim tolerance for the other because they won't tell the other person they are wrong, but deep down they believe they are wrong. If they didn't believe the other person was wrong, then they would become like them and embrace the same worldview. Yet they don't. They maintain variant worldviews and live out these diversities all while claiming the same worldview which is a lie. A Christian, however, is honest about the situation, admitting that we don't hold the same worldview and are therefore different. This claim somehow deems the Christian intolerant, even if the Christian is not treating the divergent worldview holder any more harshly than the moral relativist. If a Christian is truly living in the love of God, then he will treat the non-believer better than the other "tolerant" non-believer even as he is called intolerant. But because the Christian honestly sees the variant worldviews and recognizes that we all automatically claim a worldview whether we claim Christ or not, he is intolerant. For what? Not for his actions, but for his claim to moral Truth.

If no God exists, then no moral realm can be justified. It really is every man for himself, and all things are neutral. I can kill, rape, torture, abuse, lie, steal, gossip, slander, and the list goes on for every single action you can name, and none of it is right or wrong. Consensus may decide for the group what rules they want to follow, but no single action would innately "be" wrong.

Yet almost all of humanity feels something negative inside once they reach a certain age and do something harmful to others. If God does not exist, then this cannot be a reality? Stop and think about this hard. Do you ever naturally feel bad about something? If you were to go to your neighbor, rape and torture them before killing them, would you only feel bad because you knew the cultural group had decided that was an action they don't agree on as a rule? Or would you just naturally feel bad inside? If the latter is your truth, then maybe Truth really does exist beyond us. And if Truth really does exist beyond us, where does it come from? It must come from someone made of something different than the stuff you and I are made of. The plausible answer then is God. And if God exists, then his Truth really is the true way to live which means only one true worldview exists.

Argument Against Christianity- Claim Number 2:
Christianity is a blind faith.

Science is not my forte, so I will say now that other resources exist to better assist in this argument. Years ago, I studied some of Ken Ham's curriculum and found it to be very helpful, so if nothing else, I would urge you to google him. What I do know is that somehow non-believers readily believe that Christians are completely ignorant to "real science" and have dumbly accepted a faith that is blind to the truths that intellectual people have proven in the scientific field.

Last time I checked, science is built on theories, and by its very definition, a theory is "a supposition or a system of ideas intended to explain something, especially one based on general principles independent of the thing to be explained." Suppositions are not truths. Although scientific suppositions are based on general laws of science that have developed over the years, the discipline still requires the inquirer to come to a set of evidence and do his best to discern reality based on the evidence. The problem lies in the inquirer. If I come to a set of evidence with one worldview, my interpretations will move in a much different direction than if I come to the same set of evidence with a different worldview.

I know Christian scientists have substantial data to disprove carbon dating. I know the flood accounts for numerous anomalies within the geological evidence we see in our world. I know the biological study of human design alone fully points to a designer. Think about your eye, or your ear, or your heart, or your brain. Think about how this could just happen to all come together in the right sequences in time and space to enable human life to function as it does. Think about our universe. Think about the exact positioning of our world and how a slight difference would cause all things to fall apart. I cannot help but look at my own body and the world around me and think that anyone who refuses to acknowledge a grand designer behind all of this requires more blind faith than I do.

Argument Against Christianity- Claim Number 3:
The Christian God is not someone worthy of my allegiance.

Hurt people hurt people. Oftentimes, people are more willing to consider belief in God when they have endured a deep struggle they could not handle on their own. So, they turn to faith, but they are hurting, and even if God begins a redemptive work in them, they are still clinging to the desires of the flesh; we are all always struggling with surrendering self to the Spirit. So as each member of God's church works to build His kingdom, they are also working to become more like Him. Yet we are not yet perfected, so we fall short, and as we fall short, we hurt others along the way. This unfolds as the baseline for so many I know who reject Christ yet deeply love others, loving so big and hard and wide and long, all while finding the church to be lacking in love. Rightfully so.

God, my friends, is never lacking. Too often, we turn away from God, hurling accusations against him that are not His to claim. He is good and kind and loving and forgiving and gracious and merciful, and yet He is also a just God. Don't ever forget that all things flow together perfectly in his nature.

Some ask me how I can call God good when he allows such deep pain in this world. Free will remains my rebuttal, even as I too feel the heartbreak.

A young girl named Rylie passed away at the age of twenty-one. She had spent numerous hours in my room when she was in high school after a devastating heartbreak. I watched her walk away from any leanings toward faith and right into a secular lifestyle as she desperately grasped at anything that would make her feel whole again. As I walked into her funeral, I was heartbroken. I was heartbroken that I knew the end of her life on earth did not bring peace; I was heartbroken as I hugged student after student who had been part of my life through the years, knowing they too were facing a similar doom one of these days. It was one of the hardest days of my life.

As I sat and prayed for those aching young hearts, I begged God to open their eyes. I pleaded with Him to let them see the promise I held. I knew I could offer the only thing that would grant solace for each of them while also knowing they were all leaving that funeral to go commemorate her life with fleeting reprieves that would only leave them feeling worse in the morning. And as I left that funeral, one of her closest friends who also happened to be one of my closest students told me he would gladly go to hell. The context was different than my understanding in the moment as I later learned, but in that moment, I was devastated and furious. So, I called Dean and asked to meet with him the next day.

The next day was Sunday, and as I asked my pastor to pray for the conversation, he looked at me and said, "I love your heart." Tears streaming down my face from having expressed my deep love for this young man, loving him as if he were my own son, I told my pastor that some days I hated my heart. Some days I do. It seems too soft and too burdened and too caring...so hear me when I say that I feel pain just as deeply as you do.

Am I using God as a crutch to deal with my struggles because I am too weak to do it on my own? You bet. And if you are honest, you are too weak to do it on your own too, and if you think you aren't, then count yourself lucky I suppose because you either haven't faced real hardship yet, or your heart is too hardened to truly know pain. If the latter is you, then I actually feel really sorry for you because it must be such a lonely place to not get to experience real love. And when I say I feel sorry for you, that is an honest statement that I feel heartache for you the same as I felt heartache for all those students standing in that tear-stained funeral.

So why does God allow such deep pain? The only way He can stop it is to stop free will. If the garden of Eden story is true, and I believe it is, then the idea of choice is real. If the idea of choice is real, then humanity has always been offered two things: live for yourself or live for God. Life with God eternally means provision and love and acceptance and goodness and kindness and perfection; it means you get to stay in the Garden and eat forever from the tree of life. Life with yourself means separation from God. Because He is true to His nature and can be nothing but true, He cannot allow things untrue to His nature to be in His presence without some sort of payment. That payment is your very life, but of course, we know there is more to that story. Thank God today that He sent His very own son to be your payment so He could bridge the gap of separation, and you get to be back in community with Him again.

God wants the Garden of Eden for you, and He wants the Garden of Eden for me, but He wants us to have the freedom to choose Him; otherwise, we are nothing more than robots. Living like that is simply not love but rather enslavement. A good God would never enslave His people, even as He knows that the choice comes with a price, a very high price, and it also comes with pain for you and me along the way.

The same argument of free will answers why God allows evil, why God allows bad to sometimes reign, why God allows anything we deem unpleasant. But then again, it should strike us all as odd that the very people who are upset with God for allowing pain and evil are the same people claiming God doesn't exist and therefore no moral truth exists which should mean that pain and evil aren't real either but just a construct devised by Christians to oppress others.

Does it not seem more likely that the biggest source of oppression is humanity itself? God doesn't hurt us; people do. God doesn't oppress us; people do. God doesn't leave us to contend with the messiness of self-service but instead steps in to make a way for us. Is he just? Yes. Does that mean we will have consequences for denying Him? Yes. If he didn't have consequences for the unjust and the evil, he wouldn't be a good God. And I hope the more you come to know Him, the more you will see that He is ever and only a good, good Father.

Dear friend, we live in a culture that is working harder than ever to convince every one of us that God is dead, self is alive, and trust thyself only. I don't know about you, but I tried that road for a while. I lived a life full of me and found it be hollow and depressing. I searched high and low and still felt very, very empty. And then I came to the foot of the cross, and I laid it all down. I surrendered my life into His hands, and He filled me up. He showed me that I will never be enough on my own. He reminded me that He is always enough, and when I let His very Spirit live out my life for me, then I become a vessel for him. With

His lifeline pumping through every ounce of me, I feel more alive, more whole, more loved than words could ever express. When I decided that I could look at Him and say, "You are enough," then I would finally be able to look in the mirror and say the same. I am not enough because of me; I am enough because He lives in me, and He is enough. God, You Are Enough. YAE.

Reflection Quest:

1. Write out a letter to a nonbeliever, presenting evidence for faith. If you are an unbeliever, write the letter to yourself:).

Meet Me Here

-To Hell For Him?-

One day as I was sitting at my podium in the back of the room with Dean's seat right next to mine, we somehow began a conversation on the corners of scrap paper while both he and I should have been paying attention to the student presenter standing in the front of the classroom. Between each presentation, I would dialogue a bit more with him. I don't remember the specifics of the conversation, but I readily recall it was an apologetic debate; he argued against the reality of God while I adamantly insisted God's not dead.

Within two years, we would be sitting in my truck as I drove him around and we again debated, only this time because Rylie had just died young. He had decided that he loved others so much that he would gladly take their place and go to hell all while insisting a good God could never let her die. I don't know how much he heard of my arguments, but as I left him, I was praying he heard loud and clear that I loved him enough to not just sit back and watch him walk straight into hell. Most importantly, God loved him enough to not just sit back and watch him walk straight to hell.

Open, raw, honest, tearful conversations with a young man who just couldn't let go and let God in. But ya know, I love him deeply still. He is and always has been one of my favorite students (but don't tell him I said that:). If someday you do read this, my dearest Dean, please know I am still praying for your own personal re-vision.

ELEVEN

PAIN AND PURPOSE

Anticipation Questions:

1. Why does God allow pain?
2. Is God worthy of your praise?

Music has always been a primary pathway for communication between me and God. My family grew up watching little television but listening to much music, so I suppose that is how it all began. I still rarely watch any kind of television, but my Spotify is a close friend.

Years ago, when I had gone back to teaching full-time with a busy schedule of three smaller school children, a home, my husband's farm of endless tasks, and my church family/ministry, I was desperately seeking God's direction. I felt overwhelmed most days as I made the thirty-minute trek to work. As is my habit, I would plug in some Christian music (in the days of cd's; I am old, I know), and I would listen to God's truth, begging for some encouragement and clarity as I faced yet another day. On this morning, I put in a cd I had listened to numerous times, so nothing new should have spoken to me. But as only God can do, He was timing a moment just for me and Him.

My drive took me toward a little town called Belmont. Right before the approach to Belmont, the road climbs upward to a minor high point before descending toward the Belmont crossroads. A song by Britt Nicole called "The Sun is Rising" came on. I was going through a time where I was desperate for God to help heal my hurts and wounds and felt like I just needed a break so I could breathe. And for no other reason than God speaking to me, I heard these words for the first time, even as I had listened to the song many times before, and God spoke this into me:

> When life has cut too deep and left you hurting
> The future you had hoped for is now burning
> And the dreams you held so tight lost their meaning
> And you don't know if you'll ever find the healing

I felt my heart breaking, yearning for my students to know Jesus, longing for relationships to be fully restored, begging God to give me time to be a Godly mom to my three children. Then, just as I breached that hill leading into Belmont, these words came on at the very same moment that my vehicle sat at the highest point and the rising sun rushed over me, practically blinding me with its brightness of hope:

> Lift up your eyes and see
> The sun is rising

It was a moment I will never forget.

Immediately my eyes gushed forth tears as I knew I had just encountered God in a very real way. He had ordained the sun to rise into my vehicle at that exact same time when I would hear those words, reminding me that all I have to do is lift up my eyes to see that He is right there for me.

I called up my best friend, and between tears of joy, I shared my moment with her. I had to tell someone about this incredible encounter with God Himself. And even as my circumstances remained a deep struggle, I suddenly found new wings so I could run and not grow weary, walk and not faint. The God of the universe spoke directly to me, so how could I ever doubt His goodness and provision.

As I thought and prayed about how to write one final chapter, I knew that purpose in pain would be the mantra of God's words to you. I wish I could tell you that since that moment I have soared high above all struggles, but that would be a lie. I wish I could tell you that life is easy, but it simply is not. Life is hard, my friend.... but God is good.

I know you have heard that, but I so wish I could just sit with you so you could hear the earnest passion in my voice when I whisper God is good. He is soo good. He is my Jehovah Jireh, my intimate provider.

Even as I write this, though, you may be merely reading the words on the page. You may have a story of unredeemed pain that has convinced you there is no way it has a purpose, and if it doesn't have a purpose, then God must either be dead, or he isn't worthy of your worship. Maybe, then, you can relate to the following story and sense the deep pains within.

Once upon a time, there was a young girl named Tally. Tally was the youngest of three. Smart, athletic, popular, Tally was one of those girls who seemed to have a lot going for her. But when her senior year hit, her mom, Marie, had an accident at the local factory where Marie worked. Tally went with her dad after the factory called to let them know about Marie's head injury so she could bring her mom's car back to the house. As they got to the factory, Marie looked right at Tally and had no idea who she was. It was a moment that haunted Tally for years to come.

Fast forward twenty-seven years. By this time, Marie's head injury has onset Meniere's disease which onset diabetes which then led eventually to a whole list of medical ailments like heart failure, kidney failure, pulmonary embolisms, bone and joint deterioration, and eventually cancer. It was a slow but steady decline of one thing after another until years had stolen away Tally's mom piece by piece by piece.

Tally was the only one there in the hospital when her mom got the news about the cancer. Honestly, if she had heard the news five years prior, it would have been devastating. But ever since Tally's mom had Covid, Marie had been on an even steadier decline, and the last nine months especially had been harder yet. Marie had begun to lose a lot of weight and suffer from unexplained autonomic failure. Tally and her family had been losing their mom for too many years now for news like cancer to feel overwhelming.

When other women are celebrating the ways their moms have supported them throughout their adult years, Tally can't help but recollect all the things she lost as she had to instead carry her mom. And if you ever think the pain of watching a loved one is bearable, then try doing it for twenty-seven years.

Maybe we should pause for a quick confession.

This is my story. Tally=me/Marie=my mom. And there have been times in the last twenty-seven years that I shook my fists at God and begged him for some relief. Too many surgeries. Too many broken bones, broken ribs, broken hopes. Too many hospital stays. Too many times sitting with my mom in her bed because she was physically not able to get out of it. Too many times of picking flowers so my mom could at least see what grows in the gardens that she loves so well.

To say that life has been full of pain is an understatement. And you better believe it would be easy to react a different way, the way too many people I love react. They ask how a loving God could allow such heartache and scream foul play at Him, asserting that even if He is real, He is certainly not worthy of their praise.

Wanna know something? As hard as it was to walk the twenty-seven years with my mom, it is nothing compared to walking the past ten years with some of my students. Wanna know why it is harder with them? Because as indescribable and difficult as the pain was for my mom, she knew it has great purpose because she loved Jesus well. So one day, she and I will dance on the streets that are golden, even though it has been way too many years since I was a little girl dancing away to sweet music with my lovely mama.

But as frustrating and inexplainable as this life has been for some of my students, they refuse to see past the pain, and that means they will never hear the dance music play. For me and for my heart that aches to have them dancing with me, their denial makes all the difference.

When I ask one of my students (who is so dear to me that I would go to the ends of the earth for him) why he won't accept Christ, he tells me about his deep pains, about his job as a nurse, about the endless suffering he sees on this earth and the great lack of compassion for humankind. He tells me stories that make my heart ache, but at the end of the day, my heart aches most because he won't be in eternity with me. So, I have spent years trying to just share life with him and give intellectual reasons why God is trustworthy (largely because he is brilliant and needs something more than what seems to him to be blind faith). But the pain is too deep, and the hurt is too real, and when you choose to let the pain blot out the purpose and the promise, you lose all sight of hope.

Hope is my life word. My closest friends buy me things that say hope, knowing that it is my life's mantra. Just the other day I was talking with a non-Christian and defined hope in a brand-new way for him. Hope is desire accompanied by expectation. When I say I hope for something, I am not just casually throwing out a fleeting possibility for the future. No, my hope is built on nothing less than Jesus's blood and righteousness, the very one who knew so well the purpose behind the pain.

Your perspective determines your outcome. And the way you see the world fully dictates the way you live out your flash of a life here on earth. Too many choose to see things through the pain. I choose to see things through God's purpose, and that makes all the difference now and for eternity.

Maybe another story will help bring this point home.

The bible tells a lot of stories about a guy named Abraham, but one of my favorites is when Abraham takes Isaac up the mountain to sacrifice him. If you pay attention to details, we gather that Isaac was a robust teenager at the time. They begin their trek, and three days into the travel, Abraham tells the two servants to wait for them. Taking Isaac further along with him, Isaac asks his dad about the sacrifice, noting that they have the fire and the wood but no lamb for the burnt offering to which Abraham says, "God himself will provide the lamb for the burnt offering, my son." So, on they go. Eventually, they get to the designated spot and build an altar. Then Abraham binds Isaac, lays him on the altar, and takes out his knife to slay his son. Consider the fact that Abraham is old, Isaac is young (maybe 16-20); therefore, Isaac must trust his dad a lot because he could have easily fought him off. Isaac must also trust God a lot. If you know the story, God stops Abraham just as he is about to slay his beloved son and provides a ram in a thicket as the sacrifice.

Abraham and Isaac both had a choice. They could have had eyes full of pain throughout this test, or they could trust God to provide. Choosing the latter made all the difference; choosing to trust the purpose brought life.

Dear friend, God wants to offer you a new vision. He wants to give purpose to your pain so you can begin to see how very worthy He is of your praise. And he doesn't ask you to praise Him for his own narcissistic sake. He is already completely God and no amount of worship you bring to Him will change the fact that He is 110% complete with or without you. Why then does He ask us to worship him? It is always and only for our sake. God doesn't need you; God is so complete He needs nothing. God *wants* you, and He wants to offer you things beyond your own abilities and even your own imagination.

I heard a song recently that greatly spoke to me. Phil Wickham, in his song "It's Always Been You," declares that he longs to be in God's presence, because God alone is the voice that can calm our storm and protect us from the deep wounds that threaten to take us out. God alone is the light that shines in our darkness, and God alone will always be there for us and has always been there for us. He is the one who stands with us in the fire. He is the one who pulls us out of the water. He is the one who carries us on His shoulders. He is THE ONE. It truly has always been Him.

Dear friend, when Abraham is on that mountain with Isaac, God tells Abraham his name is Jehovah Jireh, the God who provides. Please know this isn't a-I'll send you a little help along the way now and then like throwing candy at a parade. This is intimate, close, I see you and your struggles, and I am nearer to you than the very air you are breathing, and I know your hurt, I know your pain, I know your sorrows and your questions and your doubts, and yet I am right here providing for you. All you have to do is look up.

Look up, my friend. The Son IS RISING.

You can choose to be like my students and see only the things of this earth, but that will mean that life continues to be a deep burden to bear. Or you can choose to look beyond the clouds, and I hope you have sensed through these pages that that view offers something much, much better.

Jesus himself gave up heaven to come to this messed up earth just so He could die on a cross. Purpose for the pain.

See Him. Know Him. Choose to see beyond the pain to the purpose, and it will change everything. To all my students and any of you who are struggling, I am praying for you through the tears and heartache of my love for you because of ***God's*** great love for you. And I hope you pray for me too, so I can be reminded of God's great purpose as I watch pain unfold in the time I have left here on earth. I pray that we all choose a re-vision, where we look beyond the pain, where we look to the one who holds us through it all.

Look up, child. Trust the God who provides; believe He really is Jehovah Jireh. Make a choice for how you will view everything in this world, and I will be praying you choose hope. . .Choose Him.

Meet Me Here

-The Story of My Life-

I don't know your name and I don't know your story, but God does. Before you go any further though, I encourage you to write yourself into this book. Write out where you have been so far in your journey with God. And don't be afraid to be transparent and authentic. And if you are willing, send your story my way.... apearlberry@gmail.com.

TWELVE

EPILOGUE

Where to Now...The Roman Road

When the Romans were high in power, they dominated ancient civilization for numerous years. During their reign, they built roads and became well known for them, the Appian Way being the most famous.

In the bible, there is another famous Roman Road that offers an insight into what it looks like to offer your life to God. The first stop is Romans 3:23, where we are reminded that we have all sinned and fallen short of God's glory. Every single human to walk this earth except Jesus himself have lived a life of sin, and there is nothing you or I can do to stop this truth about human nature. We mess up, and the sooner we realize it the better.

The second stop is Romans 5:8 where we then learn that God's love is so great that while we are still sinners, Christ died for us. Notice who is responsible for the shift. We are the sinners, Christ is the redeemer, which leads to stop three in Romans 6:23 (NIV) which states, "The wages of sin is death, but the gift of God is eternal life in Christ Jesus our Lord." God, in his great goodness for us, provides a way out of eternal death and damnation through his very own beloved son.

Because of God's great grace, we come to stop four which tells us we face no condemnation if we are in Christ Jesus (Romans 8:1). We are each given a choice, and when we choose to SEE God for who He is and Christ for the great salvation he offers, we gain a new identity, no longer living in fear of eternal hell. This leads us to Romans 10:9 (NIV) and our final stop: "If you confess with your mouth, 'Jesus is Lord,' and believe in your heart that God raised him from the dead, you will be saved." Confession coupled with belief renders salvation.

At this point, some would ask you to say a prayer if you are ready. Although I will certainly never tell you to not cry out to our great God, I will also say that living a life for Christ is the most beautiful thing I do but also the hardest. Does salvation require anything beyond your hearing the truth, believing Christ died for you, repenting of your self-centeredness as you beg God to give you a life of Him, confessing to others of where you've been and your decision to gain a new identity, and then being baptized in the name of the Father, Son, and Holy Spirit? Salvation really is a simple choice, so don't make that difficult. But also know that sanctification is a life-long process, so don't make that alone.

Find Godly people who will mentor you in your journey and hold you accountable, but also who will offer untold encouragement. Join the comm(on)unity of God's kingdom; please don't try to do it alone. Satan finds isolated Christians to be easy prey. It reminds me of the coyotes who frequent our farm. In the fields nearby, they anticipate an isolated foe, and when they find the unfortunate animal alone, they pack together for the attack. Satan is doing the same, watching and waiting for you to try to go it alone. Don't fall prey right out of the gate.

My prayer is you have journeyed this book with one person who is already in your corner. Keep them as a treasure, and then let them help you find more. And eventually, as you bloom into all the things God has set before you, you will shift roles as you lead others to know the real Him, and to know Him more.

Find a church family. I must warn you, however, that churches are messy. I have yet to find the perfect church because they are always filled with imperfect people...but don't let that deter you. Set out to find a community where you can worship in fellowship with other believers AND where you can serve. Our church motto/my school's motto is Love God, Love People, Serve Both. It is my prayer that you can find a place where you can get connected, where you can encounter

God while encountering community, and through it all you can learn to live a life of service. God himself spends his days at WORK; we should do the same, working diligently to build His kingdom one day at a time.

Finding community is important, but don't forget to find God along the way as well, because He is the only one who won't let you down. Pursue Him every single day of your life. A young woman I mentor has heard me say numerous times, "I pray you love God more today than you loved Him yesterday." His love is already perfect which means He cannot love us any more or any less than He already does. We, on the other hand, are tethered by our flesh and the desires of this world, so every day we get to choose to cast aside that rotting self and embrace His ways and know Him more and more until one day we finally get to go Home. Oh, what a sight that will be…for the first time, we really will see perfectly.

In the meantime, dear friend, God wants you to open your eyes as wide as you can today and see him in a brand-new way. And he wants you to do the same tomorrow and the next day and the next. I can promise you that years from now if I am still on this earth, I will reread what I have written and will see gaps and misconceptions in what I see today. I could certainly let that deter me from this writing endeavor, or I could be transparent and vulnerable to let you know that this is where my heart is today, but the last thing God wants is for my heart to stay in this place.

God yearns for my heart to become more and more like his each day, a continual growth to be more like Him. He wants the same for you.

I am praying you leave these pages with a fresh vision of what it means to be in love with God. May He alone be the source of our sight as we live our lives with eyes fixed solely on Him.

ABOUT THE AUTHOR

Lesa Shilling is Headmaster and Teacher for Mission III Academy, a private, Christian school she and her husband Daniel established in their hometown of Albion, Illinois. Through this ministry, Lesa serves numerous families in her local counties along with remote students, teaching them foremost to Love God, Love People, and Serve Both. She is the blessed mother of Nate, Katherine, and Caleb, along with numerous others who claim her as a bonus mom. Lesa earned her first bachelor's degree from Milligan College with a double-major in History and English and studied at Oxford University for a semester program during her stint at Milligan. She also holds a bachelor's degree from the University of Southern Indiana in English Education and a Master of Arts in English from Morehead State University. Lesa's passion in life is to follow the commands that Jesus gave to his disciples when He said we must all deny our "self," take up our cross, and follow Him.

Printed in the United States
by Baker & Taylor Publisher Services